CONNECTICUT

CONNECTICUT BY ROAD

CELEBRATE THE STATES
CONNECTICUT

Victoria Sherrow

BENCHMARK BOOKS

MARSHALL CAVENDISH
NEW YORK

Benchmark Books
Marshall Cavendish Corporation
99 White Plains Road
Tarrytown, New York 10591-9001

Copyright © 1998 by Marshall Cavendish Corporation

Library of Congress Cataloging-in-Publication Data
Sherrow, Victoria.
Connecticut / Victoria Sherrow.
p. cm. — (Celebrate the states)
Includes bibliographical references and index.
Summary: Surveys the geography, history, people, and customs of Connecticut.
ISBN 0-7614-0205-5 (lib. bdg.)
1. Connecticut—Juvenile literature. [1. Connecticut.] I. Title. II. Series.
F94.3.S54 1998 974.6—dc20 96-42008 CIP AC

Maps and graphics supplied by Oxford Cartographers, Oxford, England

Photo research by Ellen Barrett Dudley and Matthew J. Dudley

Cover photo: *The Image Bank*, Steve Dunwell

The photographs in this book are used by permission and through the courtesy of: *McConnell McNamara & Co.*: 6-7, 13, 14, 17, 19, 72, 113, 115, 116, 117, back cover. *The Image Bank*: Steve Dunwell, 10-11, 50; Michael Melford, 15, 132; Walter Bibikow, 25; Patti McConville, 40; Gary Gladstone, 71, 121; Guido Alberto Rossi, 79. *Photo Researchers, Inc.*: Harry Engels, 22; Tom Myers, 27; Chromosohm/Sohm, 54-55; Jerome Wexler, 74-75; Guy Gillette, 82; Del Mulkey, 110-111; M.H. Sharp, 125 (left); Bonnie Sue, 125 (right); Joseph T. Collins, 129. *Wadsworth Atheneum, Hartford*: Gift of Mr. and Mrs. Thomas L. Archibald, 28-29; Gift of Mrs. Josephine Marshall Dodge and Marshall Jewell Dodge in memory of Marshall Jewel, 37. *The Connecticut Historical Society, Hartford*: 31, 33, 41, 49, 58. *Corbis-Bettmann*: 32, 93, 94, 95, 97, 98, 99, 101, 102, 134 (top), 137 (top). *Leslie M. Newman*: 36, 51, 68, 77, 86, 87, 88 (top and bottom), 90-91, 123, 137 (bottom). *Michael Marsland/Yale University*: 39. *New Haven Colony Historical Society*: 44. *The American Clock and Watch Museum*: 48. *UPI/Corbis-Bettmann*: 59, 61, 105, 108, 135 (bottom). *Jason R. Wise*: 64, 81. *Albert Dickson/The Hartford Courant*: 65. *AP/Wide World Photos*: 106. *Secretary of State's Office*: 124 (bottom). *Reuters/Corbis-Bettmann*: 134 (bottom). *Springer/Corbis-Bettmann*: 136.

Printed in Italy

2 4 6 5 3 1

CONTENTS

CONNECTICUT IS...

Connecticut is a land of woods and rivers.

"The spring vacation came, and I went home to North Guilford [to make] maple-sugar. We had about a hundred trees. Oh, I wish you could see them now, with their great spreading roots! I used to delight in that work, tapping the trees, boiling down the sap, and carrying it home."　—Lyman Beecher, clergyman and author, 1793

"The [Connecticut River] may perhaps with as much propriety as any in the world, be named the beautiful river."
　　　—Timothy Dwight, historian and president of Yale University
　　　　from 1795 to 1815

The home of the first lollipop, Frisbee, and U.S. submarine, the state claims many pioneering inventions.

"Eli Whitney's Gun-factory, two miles north of New Haven, was the great curiosity of the neighborhood. Indeed, people traveled fifty miles to see it."　　　—Samuel G. Goodrich, inventor, 1809

"A tiny little state, devoid of natural resources, has compiled a record of human resourcefulness that warrants the admiration of all."　　　　—Homer Babbage, humorist and educator, 1978

People here like to think for themselves.

"The best thing about Connecticut people is that they ignore patterns. They are individualists, which makes it hard for politicians. . . . Connecticut, like most of New England, has a lot of free-thinkers, often cantankerous and opinionated people. And most Connecticut people prize that quality in others."

—Harrison E. Salisbury, journalist, 1989

Connecticut is looking toward the future . . .

"We're in post-industrial America. Our strategy is to reposition Connecticut as a manufacturing state."

—Joseph J. McGee, state commissioner
of economic development, 1994

. . . while treasuring what is good about the past.

In Connecticut, colonial charm meets modern industry. Old church spires, quaint village squares, and historic monuments and homes stand face-to-face with superhighways, manufacturing plants, modern sports facilities, and steel-and-glass high-rises. While some families have lived in Connecticut for centuries, many residents have only recently arrived from places around the globe.

Connecticut has changed greatly since the earliest white settlers arrived in the 1600s. But in many ways, the words of the nineteenth-century French traveler and author Alexis de Tocqueville still ring true:

> Connecticut is that little yellow spot [on the map] that makes the clock-peddlar, the schoolmaster, and the senator; the first gives you the time, the second tells you what to do with your time, and the third makes your law and your civilization. This little yellow state you call Connecticut is one very great miracle to me.

1 NATURAL WONDERS

Clipper, Mystic Seaport

That little . . . spot, Connecticut, is the third-smallest state in the United States, after Rhode Island and Delaware. Shaped like a small rectangle, the state sits at the southernmost point of New England. It is bordered by New York on the west, Rhode Island on the east, and Massachusetts on the north.

Except for a narrow coastal plain, there is little flat or empty land in the state's 5,018 square miles. Waterways, hills, deep forests, ravines, and rocks dot the landscape. The Connecticut River Valley lowland runs north into Massachusetts and offers the best farmland in the state. In the west and east rise the New England uplands, with the Taconic Mountains in the northwest. Long Island Sound, an arm of the Atlantic Ocean, borders Connecticut to the south. The land rises gradually from the long sandy beaches and small wooded islands of this shoreline.

PLENTIFUL WATERS

Access to water has strongly influenced where people have settled in Connecticut. Three major river systems enabled people to move about and to transport goods from place to place: the Connecticut, the Housatonic, and the Thames. Ships docked easily along the ocean coastline, linking Connecticut to ports around the country and the world. Water also provided energy for industry and fish for food.

Cows graze at Glastonbury Farm. Nineteenth-century farmers made a durable red paint from iron oxide to brighten their barns.

These waterways drew European settlers to the region during the 1600s. In 1680, colonists praised New London, the finest sheltered harbor on the coast. They wrote to officials in England: "Ships of great [size] may com up to the town and lye secure in any winds." Of the New London (Pequot) River, they said, "a ship of 500 tunn may go up to the Towne, and com so near the shore that they may toss a biskit ashoare: and vessells of about 30 tunn may pass up about 12 miles above N. London . . ." [sic]

In all, Connecticut has 8,400 miles of rivers and streams. The Connecticut River, the longest in New England, rises near the Canadian border and forms a boundary between New Hampshire and Vermont. It flows across western Massachusetts and central Connecticut before reaching Long Island Sound at Old Saybrook.

The Essex River flows into the southern part of the Connecticut River near Long Island Sound.

Tobacco, seen here at Windsor Locks, has been grown in the state for hundreds of years.

Along the Connecticut River Valley is some of the most fertile land east of the Mississippi. Farmers grow potatoes, corn, onions, asparagus, tomatoes, lettuce, hay, and a few thousand acres of tobacco, which is used for cigar wrappers. The Housatonic River waters western Connecticut, while the Thames River flows through the eastern part of the state.

More than one thousand lakes are strewn across the state's surface. Most of them were formed thousands of years ago when the glaciers that had covered the land during the Ice Age melted. One of the largest is Barkhamsted Reservoir in the north, with its man-made dam. Glaciers also sculpted the earth to form ridges and polished layers of rocks.

ROCKS

Connecticut soil is full of rocks, some of which date back about four hundred million years. Sandstone and shale abound in the Connecticut River Valley. Traprock, which is quite hard, has been used for roads. Clay deposits, employed in making brick, lie in the Quinnipiac and Housatonic Valleys. From western Connecticut comes limestone, used to build homes and to grind into plaster for walls. Connecticut supplied granite for the foundation of the Statue of Liberty and brownstone (a dark sandstone) for buildings in New York City.

To early farmers, though, these rocks were nothing but a back-breaking burden. Day after day, settlers dug rocks from their fields to make room for crops. They fashioned piles of rocks into stone fences, which marked the boundaries of their property and kept the neighbors' cows away from their ripening corn. Stone walls, both old and new, are still a common—and charming—sight in this New England state.

WOODS

Connecticut was once almost entirely covered with woods. Today, it is about 60 percent forest, making it one of America's most heavily wooded states. Many wooded acres are protected from commercial development. Ninety-one state parks cover more than

Many stone fences divide fields and wind along roads in rural and suburban Connecticut.

A SPELUNKER'S DELIGHT

Spelunkers—people who explore caves—have much to see in Connecticut. The state has more than 275 underground spaces that qualify as caves. Some lie beneath the ground; others can be entered through the sides of hills, cliffs, or mountains.

Inside these caves are interesting lime formations, such as stalactites (which drip from the tops of caves) and stalagmites (which extend up from the floors). Bats, bears, and coyotes make their homes in caves, as do lizards, crayfish, and other creatures. They survive on water that drips into these underground spaces and by eating other living things and their eggs. Fish may also live in caves that contain enough water or underground streams.

Over the years, a few legendary people have been known to live in the state's caves. One famous example was a mysterious woman named Sarah Bishop. During the 1800s, Bishop lived in a cave rather than in the outside world, which she viewed as sinful.

thirty thousand acres. Among the many conservation areas is the 840-acre Charles E. Wheeler Wildlife Management Area at the mouth of the Housatonic River where it empties into Long Island Sound. A salt marsh and tidal flats are nearby.

Trees are the centerpiece of Connecticut's magnificent scenery. "I always enjoy seeing the leaves change color every autumn," says an eighty-three-year-old resident of Fairfield. Residents and visitors alike enjoy the brilliant shades of red, gold, and orange that adorn elms, maples, oaks, and other deciduous trees each fall.

Tapping maple trees for syrup and sugar, common in earlier times, is still done. The state produces twelve thousand gallons of maple syrup annually. During late February or early March, groups of schoolchildren visit farms to see how maple syrup is made. In the fall, visitors to farms throughout the state pay a fee to pick bags of apples for cooking and eating or to buy pumpkins for Halloween.

Various coniferous trees, including pines, cedars, and hemlocks, also abound. December finds many Connecticut families searching tree farms for the perfect Christmas tree and holiday greens.

Basketfuls of freshly picked apples are ready to be eaten raw or made into pies, cakes, crisps, cobblers, and sauce.

CLIMATE

"If you don't like Connecticut weather, just wait a minute. It will change," joked the popular author Mark Twain (Samuel Clemens). Twain, who lived in Connecticut for thirty years, observed that a rainy day often turns sunny, while a warm, dry day might end with chilly rain.

New England is known for harsh winters, but Connecticut has a humid, continental climate, somewhat milder than that of its neighbors. Temperatures rarely rise above ninety-five degrees in the summer or dip below zero in the winter. However, there are exceptions. During the famous blizzard of 1888, for instance, four feet of snow fell within thirty-six hours! Tornados and hurricanes are rare, but from spring through fall, storms are fairly common, bringing winds that strew leaves and branches across Connecticut's streets and lawns.

Residents experience four distinct seasons. The colorful leaves of autumn give way to wintry branches dripping with icicles. Frozen ponds beckon to ice-skaters, while snowy hills attract sledders and skiers. Spring is a time of blossoming dogwood trees and chattering birds. Summer brings bright flowers to woods and gardens and sunny afternoons at pools, lakes, and beaches.

PLANTS AND ANIMALS

With a seacoast, many waterways, and much forested land within its borders, Connecticut is home to a variety of plants and animals. The state is known for its wildflowers, including colorful orchids, pyrola (wintergreen), Indian pipe, and mountain laurel. Cardinal flowers decorate the woods along river valleys.

LAND AND WATER

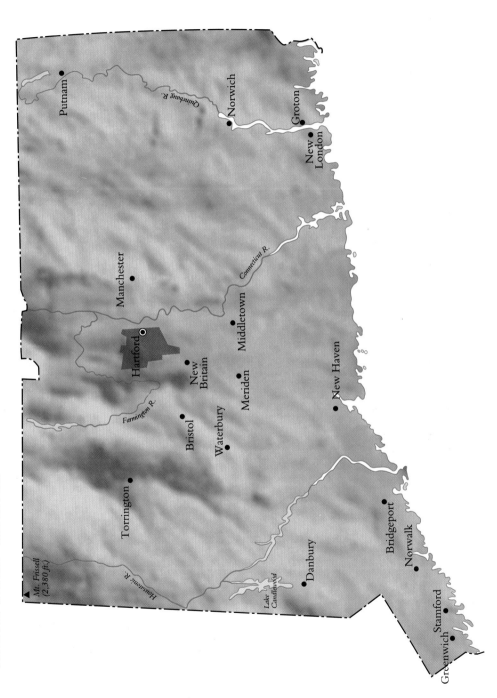

Mt. Frissell
(2,380 ft.)

Putnam

Quinebaug R.

Norwich

Groton

New
London

Manchester

Connecticut R.

Hartford

Middletown

New
Britain

Meriden

New Haven

Farmington R.

Bristol

Waterbury

Torrington

Bridgeport

Norwalk

Housatonic R.

Danbury

Lake
Candlewood

Stamford

Greenwich

Connecticut's muskrats build their homes in slow-moving water or along riverbanks.

Millions of years ago, dinosaurs roamed the Connecticut River Valley, leaving behind fossil tracks that intrigue modern-day scientists. Now, smaller animals inhabit the state. People living near wooded areas are apt to find squirrels, chipmunks, woodchucks, skunks, and raccoons in their yard. Motorists on country roads must watch out for deer, wild turkeys, and Canada geese.

Native birds include cardinals, whose bright red feathers are a welcome sight each winter. Warblers, sparrows, thrushes, and robins can be heard singing in many parts of Connecticut. The bald eagle, an endangered bird, still lives in the state. Eagles can be seen at an observation area located in Southbury.

Gulls and green herons frequent the beaches of Long Island Sound. Sociable seagulls approach people, looking for food. One family was cooking dinner at Compo Beach in Westport when a gull swooped down to snatch a hot dog from their barbecue pit!

The waterways have long been a source of food and sport fish. Trout, bass, carp, and American shad are the most common fish. During the Revolutionary War, shad was packed in barrels and fed to the troops. Tons of this fish were also exported from Connecticut to other states and to Europe. New Englanders called shad "poor man's food" because it was so plentiful.

Until the nineteenth century, salmon lived in the Connecticut River, and thousands were caught each year. Newly constructed dams prevented them from reaching their usual spawning grounds. By 1814, the salmon runs had ended.

One unwelcome resident is the tick that carries the disease named for the town of Lyme. This bacterial illness was first identified there in 1975. As small as a poppy seed, these ticks live on deer and mice, which are often found in wooded areas. Cases of Lyme disease have increased during the 1990s. People have been warned to protect themselves when they are outdoors during tick season and to check themselves carefully for bites. Scientists have developed a vaccine that protects dogs from Lyme disease and are working on a vaccine for humans.

CARING FOR THE LAND AND WATER

Though small in size, Connecticut is the fourth most densely populated state in the nation, with 3,287,116 people as of 1990. Most of these people hold jobs in manufacturing, service, and wholesale and retail trades.

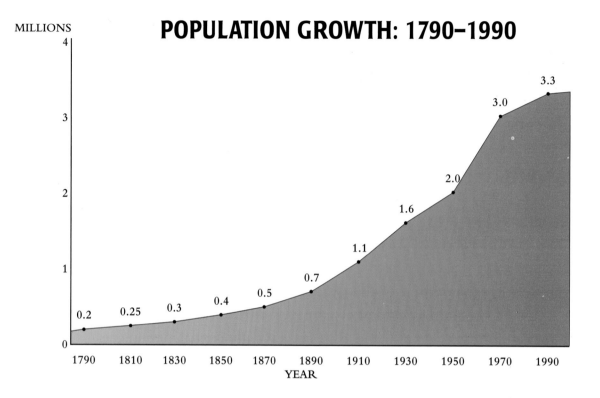

POPULATION GROWTH: 1790–1990

MILLIONS

0.2 0.25 0.3 0.4 0.5 0.7 1.1 1.6 2.0 3.0 3.3

YEAR

As Connecticut's population has grown, so has the demand for more clean water, electric power, and expanded sewage systems. The growth of industry has required using more cars, trains, and trucks. This has led to increased pollution of rivers and streams and the waters of Long Island Sound.

Many people in Connecticut care about preserving clean air and water. Pollution has long plagued the Connecticut River. As mills and factories were erected, industrial wastes flowed into the Connecticut from ditches and pipes. Dams and dikes, built to keep the river from flooding, reduced the ability of the water to cleanse itself and to fertilize the surrounding land.

As long ago as 1884, one worried conservationist from Manchester, Connecticut, complained, "A land with its rivers running filth instead of pure water, is like a body with its veins running filth instead of pure blood."

Citizens, legislators, and businesses worked together to clean up the Connecticut River, preserve wildlife and save forests and wetlands. Towns improved their sewage treatment plants. During the 1960s and 1970s federal antipollution laws became stricter.

Hartford, which lies along the Connecticut River, is an important manufacturer of aircraft engines, machinery, and metal products. Its factories provide many jobs, but they also dump waste into the river.

Parts of the river were designated as national park areas. These efforts have succeeded. By the 1990s, the river was cleaner. People could swim there again.

In the late 1960s, other man-made changes threatened the life of the river. Steam generators at nuclear power plants sent heated water into the river, raising its temperature by ten degrees or more. Scientists began studying how this could affect fish.

Former U.S. Senator and state governor Abraham Ribicoff led cleanup efforts. He said, "I love the Connecticut, not only for what it is but for what we learn about America from it. We must save what is beautiful while there is still time."

Most recently, environmentalists have focused on the 577 miles of Connecticut and New York coastline that form Long Island Sound. There, salt water from the ocean mingles with freshwater from rivers and streams. Because of pollution, fish were dying, and harbor seals were moving away. Fewer than half of the productive shellfish beds in the sound could be safely harvested. At times, beaches were closed to swimmers because of disease-causing organisms in the water.

Keeping the sound clean is difficult. As Terry Backer, Long Island Soundkeeper and director of the Soundkeeper Fund, has said, "There are millions of people living along the shore here, with cities shoulder to shoulder." The numerous sewage treatment plants in the region send nitrogen into the water. More nitrogen comes from the fertilizers people use on their lawns and gardens, some of which reaches coastal waters. Nitrogen causes algae to grow. The heavy algae plants sink in the water and break down, consuming oxygen that fish and shellfish need to live.

In 1995, federal and state agencies joined with universities, environmental agencies, businesses, and the public to form the Comprehensive Conservation and Management Plan for Long Island Sound. Congress approved a $1.5 billion Clear Water/Clean Air Act that provides $200 million for cleanup efforts. By summer 1996, some of these funds had been used to enlarge and update six sewage treatment plants. New measures controlled discharges from boats.

Like other states, Connecticut continues to seek a balance between caring for the environment, meeting the needs of its people, and maintaining a sound economy. Challenges are not new to a state that has been forced to rely more on creativity than on natural resources. People in the state have learned to be resourceful and to "make do," using their Yankee ingenuity.

Many harbor seals, native to Long Island Sound, have left due to polluted waters.

2 INDEPENDENT SPIRIT

Connecticut Landscape, by Wilson Irvine

Thousands of years before Europeans reached North America, present-day Connecticut was occupied by woodland tribes belonging to the Algonquian-speaking group. By 1600, up to twenty thousand Native Americans lived there, mostly along the coast and in the fertile river valleys. The Pequot were the dominant tribe, having conquered most of the Connecticut River Valley during the 1500s. The Narragansett and Saukiog were also large and influential tribes.

These Indians built wigwams and longhouses from sapling frames, which they covered with bark, branches, and reeds. Besides growing corn, beans, and squash, they hunted for moose, deer, and bears in the forests, along with wild turkeys and smaller fowl. They caught fish in the region's many rivers and lakes and gathered shellfish along the coast.

EARLY SETTLEMENTS

The Dutch explorer Adriaen Block met peaceful Podunk Indians when he sailed up the Connecticut River in 1614. The river emptied into Long Island Sound. Since the sound was not very deep and opened to the sea on the east, the region would be good for trade, the main interest of the Dutch.

In 1633, Dutch settlers built the House of Good Hope trading post on the river near present-day Hartford and traded with Indians

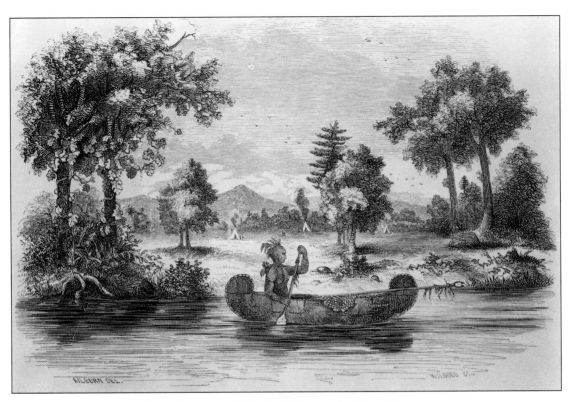

This engraving shows how Hartford looked to an early settler.

for beaver pelts. In that same year, English settlers founded present-day Windsor. Other English and Dutch settlers followed.

Friendly relations between settlers and Pequots turned violent over land disputes in 1637. The colonists, with their metal armor, muskets, and swords, quickly defeated the Indians in the Pequot War. English soldiers and colonists killed six hundred men, women, and children in the village of Mystic by setting this village of seventy wigwams on fire.

In 1638, New Haven was founded by Puritans, a conservative Protestant group from England that had been living in Massachusetts. About two hundred fifty people from Boston paid the Indians

A British ship from Plymouth sails by the Dutch trading post at Good Hope.

for the land with twenty-four knives, twenty-three coats, twelve spoons, twelve hatchets, and some scissors and garden hoes.

The New Haven government was based on a set of laws they called the Fundamental Agreement. The Bible was the supreme law for the colony. The Puritans banned long hair on men and fancy clothing. On Sunday, people could only leave home to attend church or religious meetings. People who broke laws could be severely punished, even put to death. Only Puritans could vote or hold office.

A DOCUMENT FOR FREEDOM

In 1639, residents of Wethersfield, Windsor, and Hartford formed the Colony of Connecticut. Unlike New Haven Colony, their government was based on a remarkable document inspired by Reverend Thomas Hooker. He said that citizens should be able to choose their own leaders, who would then have to account for their actions.

People discussed Hooker's ideas, and a large group of colonists approved laws they called the Fundamental Orders on January 14, 1639. This was the first document in America to say that a government gets its power from "the free consent of the people." It gave Connecticut one of its names, the Constitution State.

In later years, the Fundamental Orders inspired others, including

Reverend Thomas Hooker and his congregation are making their way through the woods with all their possessions to found a colony at Hartford.

CONNECTICUT YANKEE PEDDLERS

During the 1700s, most people in Connecticut lived on farms. They looked forward to a visit from traveling peddlers who brought horse carts filled with cloth, scissors, needles, combs, hats, and cookware to their homes. As one observer noted, "Shining coffee pots were crammed with spools of thread, papers of pins, cards of horn buttons, and cakes of shaving soap—and bolts of gaudy [ribbon] could be drawn from the pepper-boxes and sausage-stuffers."

"Connecticut Yankee peddlers," as they were called, had a reputation as clever traders. Colonial housewives liked to flavor their food with nutmeg, an imported spice. Some shady peddlers carved small, hard wooden "nutmegs" and sold them to customers, who later discovered the trick. Old stories about wooden nutmegs gave Connecticut its most amusing nickname, "The Nutmeg State."

Old tales about these tricky peddlers abound. In one story, a Yankee peddler is riding with some folks on a stagecoach out west. One passenger tells the others, "We're nearing Camden, the next stop."

"Glad to hear it," says the peddler. "I'm hungry as a dog."

"Too bad," the man tells him. "You'll get only a few mouthfuls before the stagecoach comes back for us. If you try to finish eating, you'll lose your seat."

The Yankee just grins. "I'll bet you all a free supper that I finish my meal and

Thomas Jefferson, who later wrote much of the Declaration of Independence, and James Madison, who wrote a great deal of both the U.S. Constitution and the Bill of Rights.

A GROWING COLONY

Many settlers arrived in Connecticut during the late 1600s. Relations between Native Americans and whites were mostly peaceful, and trade flourished. Colonists grew corn, flax, rye, barley, peas, and wheat; they raised sheep and cows and made cloth from wool and still keep my seat."

Once in Camden, the passengers hurry to the inn. The innkeeper charges fifty cents apiece for supper, but they are too hungry to fuss. They no sooner start eating when the innkeeper calls out, "Stagecoach is here! Driver won't wait but a minute."

Everyone rushes out, all but the Yankee. He keeps on eating and even asks for some bread pudding.

"You'll lose your seat," warns the innkeeper.

The Yankee shrugs and asks for a spoon.

"There's plenty on the table—real silver, too," the man replies.

"Hmm," says the Yankee, looking all around. "You don't suppose those folks took off with 'em, seeing as they paid so much money for only a few bites of supper?"

"Thunderation!" yells the innkeeper and storms outside.

The Yankee finishes eating, then walks outside. A big, noisy crowd has gathered near the stagecoach, and the Camden sheriff is standing beside the passengers. The sheriff comes up to the Yankee and says, "Kindly point out the thieves."

The peddler scratches his chin and looks at the innkeeper. "Seems I was mistaken," he says. "If you go look in your coffeepot, you'll find all your spoons. And thanks for a mighty fine meal!" And that's how one clever Yankee outwitted an innkeeper who liked to charge folks for food they didn't have time to eat.

flax. Using animal fat and ashes gathered from their fireplaces, they made soap every spring. Children often had to stir the soap for hours as it bubbled in a large kettle over an outdoor fire.

Young people also worked in the fields, growing and harvesting crops. While planting corn seeds, children often sang this old rhyme:

> *One for the bug,*
> *One for the crow,*
> *One to rot,*
> *And two to grow.*

Burrow's Hill Schoolhouse was built in Hebron during the 1740s. This restored one-room school is now open to visitors.

In 1650, the colony passed a law requiring every town of more than fifty families to run an elementary school. Those with more than one hundred families had to provide a secondary school, too. In these one-room schools, one teacher helped students of all ages. Schools had few books. Children learned to read by using a slate with the alphabet written on one side. They recited their lessons aloud and had regular spelling contests. Today, visitors to The Little Red Schoolhouse in Simsbury and other towns can see these colonial schools.

THE CHARTER OAK

In 1661, John Winthrop Jr., the first official governor of the Connecticut colony, visited King Charles II in London with an unusual request: Would the king recognize the colony's form of government? The king agreed, granting the colony a charter in 1662 that permitted self-rule.

After King Charles died in 1685, his brother, King James, revoked this charter, the only one of its kind in America. Edmund Andros, acting on behalf of the Duke of York, claimed the area west of the Connecticut River as part of New York colony. He declared himself governor of New England.

In October 1687, Andros went to Hartford and demanded that Governor Robert Treat give him the charter. A big meeting was held one evening by the light of many candles. Just as the charter was brought out and shown to Andros, the candles suddenly went out. Colonists smuggled the charter out a window and hid it inside the hollow of a nearby oak tree. Andros was forced to leave empty-handed. In 1689, Connecticut resumed its self-rule by charter.

The Charter Oak, as the tree became known, was cherished as a monument until a storm destroyed it in 1856. A special marker shows the spot in Hartford where this symbolic tree once stood.

The Charter Oak, by Charles DeWolf Brownell, 1857

The founders of New Haven dreamed of a fine college to educate their leaders. The town could not afford one, though. In 1700, Reverend John Pierpont organized a group to collect funds for a new college. Ten clergymen were the first trustees. By 1716, a permanent building was completed in New Haven.

Elihu Yale, who had once lived in Boston, sent the new college books from England, where his family now lived. Yale also sent shipments of goods, which the trustees could sell to raise funds for the school. The college, which the trustees named Yale in his honor, is now considered one of the finest universities in the world.

A visitor in the early 1700s noted Connecticut's "numerous towns, villages, and hamlets, almost everywhere exhibiting marks of prosperity and improvement; the rare appearance of decline; the numerous churches lifting their spires . . . , the neat school houses, every where occupied; and the mills, busied on such a multitude of streams. It may be safely asserted, that a pleasanter journey will rarely be found than that, which is made in the Connecticut Valley."

By the late 1700s, people from France, Scotland, and Ireland had joined the English and Dutch in the colony, often working as farmers and fishermen. A child walking the streets of Hartford would pass the shops of carpenters, tanners, shoemakers, coopers, blacksmiths, and tailors. Windows displayed hats, cabinets, jewelry, silver, candles, and clocks.

Some of the homes built by the colonists are standing today. Buttolph-Williams House in Wethersfield was one of the finest houses in the area during the 1600s. The kitchen has a large collection of original furnishings. Elegant Elmwood in Windsor,

New Haven's Yale University is the third-oldest institution of higher learning in the nation. Its library is among the world's finest.

built in 1740, contains a tapestry given to the family by the French Emperor Napoleon. Restored houses in Greenwich date back to the early 1700s. The Bush-Holley House sponsors History Week each year, and children can try their hand at colonial chores such as baking, sewing, and sheepshearing.

A mill house in Essex, a center for shipbuilding during the early 1800s, hugs the bank of the river.

FIGHTING FOR FREEDOM

During the Revolutionary War, from 1775 to 1783, Connecticut sent more soldiers (in relation to its population) than any other colony. About thirty thousand men from the colony fought for the Revolutionary Army, second in number only to Massachusetts, which had a larger population.

General George Washington called Connecticut the "Provisions State" because it sent so many supplies to the army. In 1777, Hartford sent thirty thousand dollars to buy supplies for Washington's troops. The following year, during the harsh winter at Valley Forge, Pennsylvania, Connecticut governor Jonathan Trumbull

Troops march through the town of Concord, Massachusetts, in 1775. Soldiers from Connecticut fought in every major battle of the Revolutionary War.

shipped the Revolutionary Army thousands of barrels of pork and beef by ox sled.

Connecticut also helped to lead the Americans to victory at sea. The colony's small navy captured more than forty British vessels. The first American submarine, a one-person vessel called the *Turtle*, was built by David Bushnell of Saybrook in 1776. The craft failed to blow up a British ship in New York Harbor as planned, but submarines would play a key role in future wars. Today, visitors to Captain's Cove Seaport in Bridgeport can see the restored British frigate, the *Rose,* the only Revolutionary warship of its kind afloat.

In 1782, General Washington created a medal he called the Purple Heart for bravery in battle. The first three men to receive it were from Connecticut. Washington cited their "daring" and "unusual gallantry."

In all, about three hundred black soldiers from Connecticut served in the Colonial Army. A prominent member of the all-black Second Company of the Fourth Regiment was Patrick Jeff Liberty. His bravery was commemorated with a monument. Jordan Freeman gave his life at Fort Griswold. He attacked a British soldier who had just killed his commander, Colonel Ledyard, after Ledyard surrendered. British soldiers led by Benedict Arnold, a Connecticut war hero turned traitor, killed Freeman and the other Americans at the fort.

AFRICAN AMERICANS

By the mid-1700s, from three to five thousand African Americans, most of them slaves, were living in Connecticut. There were no large plantations to make slavery profitable, as it was in the South. The few African Americans who were free had no political rights and were subject to the "black codes" enacted in the late 1600s. These codes required free blacks to pay taxes but banned them from voting, holding public office, and serving on a jury. Free blacks formed a separate society and elected their own governor.

By the 1700s, a growing number of white citizens opposed slavery. In 1774 a law was passed that banned bringing new slaves into the colony.

After the Revolutionary War, slaves who had been soldiers were freed. In 1784, the Connecticut Emancipation Law said that any child born to slaves would be free at age twenty-five. By 1800, 80 percent of all blacks in the state were free.

A dramatic incident involving slavery touched the state in 1839. A group of captive Africans, many of them from the Mende people, were en route to Cuba on the Spanish-owned slave ship *Amistad*. On July 1, they rebelled and killed some crew members. They told the slave traders to take them back to Africa, but, instead, the Spaniards headed toward America.

In August, the *Amistad* approached Long Island, where it was seized and taken to New London, Connecticut. Joseph Cinqué (also written Singbe-Pieh), leader of the mutiny, and his fellow Africans were accused of murder and piracy and taken to court at Hartford, Connecticut. To defend them, abolitionists—people who opposed slavery—hired well-known lawyers to take their case. These men argued that the Africans were kidnap victims, not slaves, when they rebelled.

In January 1840, Judge Andrew Judson ruled in favor of the

Africans. He declared that they had been "born free, and ever since have been and still of right are free and not slaves." Their mutiny was a desperate act of self-defense.

The decision was appealed and reached the U.S. Supreme Court in 1841. Although five of the justices were southerners who owned slaves, they agreed with Judson's decision. The Africans were allowed to return home.

PART OF A NEW NATION

Connecticut became the fifth state in the union on January 9, 1788, when residents approved the United States Constitution. Roger Sherman, who helped write the Declaration of Indepen-

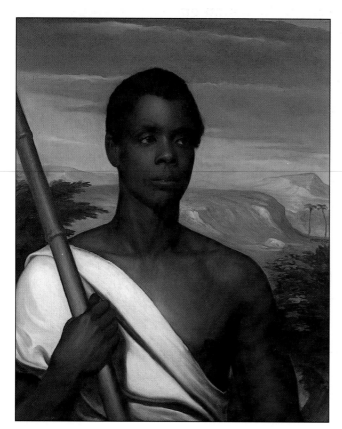

Joseph Cinqué, leader of the Amistad *rebels. Their case aided the fight against slavery, which was banned in Connecticut in 1848.*

dence, also contributed to the Constitution. He and Oliver Ellsworth proposed the "Connecticut Compromise," which allowed each state to elect the same number of senators (two) to the U.S. Congress while sending different numbers of representatives based on the population.

The early 1800s saw steady economic growth. Factories made cotton thread, woolen cloth, and paper, among other things. During this century, Connecticut's rail system, used for transporting goods, became the most complete in the nation.

"Yankee ingenuity" spurred manufacturing. Samuel Colt of Hartford made the first repeating pistol, the six-shooter, and opened a factory to produce these guns, which were widely used on the Western frontier.

In 1793, Eli Whitney invented the cotton gin. Cotton crops became much more profitable once people could use gins to remove the seeds faster. This led to increased use of slaves for farming cotton in the south.

Whitney also started a gun factory at present-day Hamden, Connecticut. His machines were among the first to make identical parts. Now when a part broke, a customer could replace it right away instead of waiting for someone to make it by hand. The introduction of assembly lines, tried by both Whitney and Colt, led to modern methods of mass production that made goods cheaper to manufacture.

Charles Goodyear of Naugatuck found a way to strengthen rubber through a process called vulcanization. In Stamford, Linus Yale invented the first modern lock in 1848. Other factories made tools and sewing machines. The first American bicycle was built

THE BATTLE OF STONINGTON

On the morning of August 9, 1814, during the War of 1812, a British naval squadron under Commodore Thomas Hardy appeared off Stonington. Hardy ordered the town authorities to have the place vacated, as it would be destroyed in an hour. When the British began the bombardment, the local militia returned fire with a few old cannon so effectively that after three days the British were forced to withdraw.

By Philip Freneau

Three gal-lant ships from Eng-land came, Freight-ed deep with fire and flame, And oth-er things we need not name, To have a dash at Ston-ing-ton. Now safe ar-rived, they work be-gun; they tho't to make the Yank-ees run, And

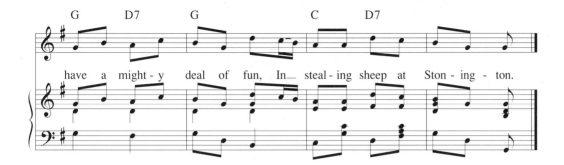

have a might-y deal of fun, In steal-ing sheep at Ston-ing-ton.

The *Ramilies* first began the attack,
And *Nimrod* made a mighty crack,
And none can tell what kept them back
From setting fire to Stonington.
Their bombs were thrown, their rockets
  flew,
And not a man of all their crew,
Though every man stood full in view,
Could kill a man of Stonington.

They killed a goose, they killed a hen,
Three hogs they wounded in a pen;
They dashed away—and pray, what
  then?
That was not taking Stonington.
The shells were thrown, the rockets flew,
But not a shell of all they threw,
Though every house was in full view,
Could burn a house in Stonington.

To have a turn we thought but fair.
We Yankees brought two guns to bear,
And, sir, it would have made you stare
To have seen the smoke at Stonington.
We bored the *Nimrod* through and
  through,
And killed and mangled half her crew,
When, riddled, crippled, she withdrew
And cursed the boys of Stonington.

The *Ramilies* then gave up the fray,
And with her comrades sneaked away;
Such was the valor on that day
Of British tars at Stonington.
Now, some assart on sartin grounds,
Beside their damage and their wounds,
It cost the king ten thousand pounds
To have a fling at Stonington.

This Victorian shelf clock was made in Bristol, about 1853.

in Connecticut, and the state became known for its fine clocks after Eli Terry set up a factory in 1804.

Today, you can see both these early timepieces and later ones at the American Clock and Watch Museum in Bristol's Miles Lewis House. More than three thousand clocks made after the year 1790 are on display. Along with plain wooden ones, there are clocks with nursery-rhyme characters, cartoon favorites, and animals. One grandfather clock is a towering ten feet tall.

In towns and cities near the sea, shipbuilding became a key industry. Sailors in search of whale oil set out from these ports. The largest fleets sailed from Mystic, Stonington, and New London. By 1860, many of the whales had been killed, and petroleum began to replace whale oil for use in lamps. By 1889, only three whaling ships remained in the state.

A nineteenth-century whaling village has been re-created at

Mystic Seaport, located beside the Mystic River. In the harbor, you can climb aboard whaling vessels for a closer look at the decks and cabins. Visitors can put on wigs, hats, aprons, or eye patches and play the part of sea captains, crew members, or pirates in outdoor historical plays.

CIVIL WAR YEARS

During the Civil War, Connecticut sent 57,379 recruits—five times more than the Union Army had expected from such a small state. These men fought at Bull Run, Gettysburg, and Antietam. More

More than one hundred whaling vessels such as this one filled Connecticut ports during the early 1800s.

Boys, dressed as drummers for the Union troops, sit by as a reenacted Civil War battle rages in Lebanon, Connecticut.

Visitors to Mystic Seaport can experience the sights and sounds of a nineteenth-century whaling village.

than twenty thousand died or were wounded or missing in action. General Ulysses S. Grant was surrounded by an honor guard of the First Connecticut Volunteers when he accepted the surrender of Confederate General Robert E. Lee. At war's end, the first Union soldiers to reach Richmond were the all-black Twenty-ninth Regiment from Connecticut.

A NEW CENTURY

By 1900, Connecticut had in many ways left behind its Puritan origins and farming ways. Immigration had brought people from all over Europe, including Irish who left during the potato famines of the mid-1800s. People arrived from Scandinavia and Germany, then from the Mediterranean and Eastern Europe. They sought economic opportunity and religious freedom.

Over the years, immigrants moved inland from the coast, especially to manufacturing towns with waterpower, harbors, and railways. The largest of these were New Haven, Bridgeport, Danbury, Waterbury, New Britain, Hartford, and Norwich. By 1900, ten towns did two-thirds of all the state's manufacturing and were home to about half of the state's residents.

TURBULENT TIMES

Since its economy relied on industry, Connecticut was hard hit by the Great Depression of the 1930s. World War II boosted the economy. Workers made airplanes, guns, submarines, and helicopters for England and France, who began fighting Germany in 1939. The demand soared after America entered the war in December 1941. Connecticut produced more war goods per person than any other state.

After the war, in the late 1940s, more than half of the state's workers had factory jobs. The economy has changed with the times. Since the 1950s, the textile industry has been dwindling. Defense-industry jobs decreased in the late 1980s when political changes led to decreased production of military weapons. As a result, electronics, machine-tool, and service-oriented businesses have become more important to the economy.

The state is known for its many small- and medium-sized businesses. In the workforce, as well as in other areas of life, Connecticut continues to adjust as it steps into the twenty-first century.

3 LAND OF STEADY HABITS

The state capitol in Hartford

Early on, people in Connecticut showed their independence. The Fundamental Orders and the unique charter of 1662 show that people wanted a democratic government that protects citizens from oppressive leaders. Respect for freedom and creative ideas have endured. These attitudes and a skilled workforce have boosted the state's economy.

INSIDE GOVERNMENT

State government in Connecticut has three branches: executive, legislative, and judicial.

Executive. The governor is the chief executive of the state, elected to a four-year term by a majority of voters in a general election. Governors initiate legislation, prepare an annual budget for the General Assembly, and appoint people to various positions. The governor lives in a nineteen-room mansion in Hartford, the state capital.

Connecticut, nicknamed the Land of Steady Habits in colonial days, has often stuck with its favorite leaders. Until recent years, there was no limit on the number of terms a governor could serve, and some served ten years or more. For instance, John Winthrop Jr., founder of New London, was governor of the colony from 1657 to 1675.

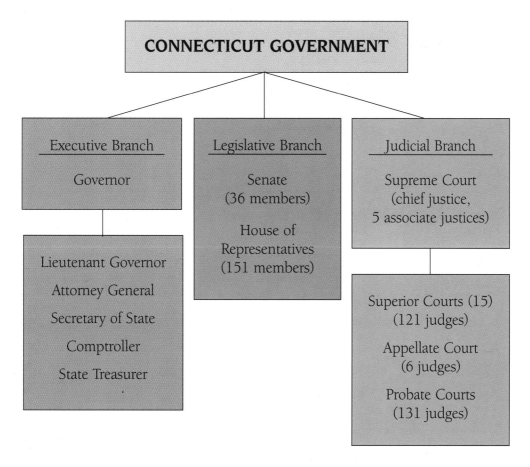

CONNECTICUT GOVERNMENT

Executive Branch

Governor

Lieutenant Governor

Attorney General

Secretary of State

Comptroller

State Treasurer

Legislative Branch

Senate
(36 members)

House of
Representatives
(151 members)

Judicial Branch

Supreme Court
(chief justice,
5 associate justices)

Superior Courts (15)
(121 judges)

Appellate Court
(6 judges)

Probate Courts
(131 judges)

Later, Jonathan Trumbull served, from 1769 to 1784. Trumbull was the only colonial governor to stay in office throughout the Revolutionary War and the first one chosen by the American people rather than by an English king.

Faith Trumbull, like her husband, became known for her patriotism during the war. One Sunday at church, the minister told the congregation how desperately the Colonial Army needed supplies. She inspired others by handing over her costly fur-trimmed cloak, a gift from a French diplomat.

Jonathan and Faith had two sons. Jonathan Trumbull II was a U.S. senator and governor of Connecticut, and his brother, John,

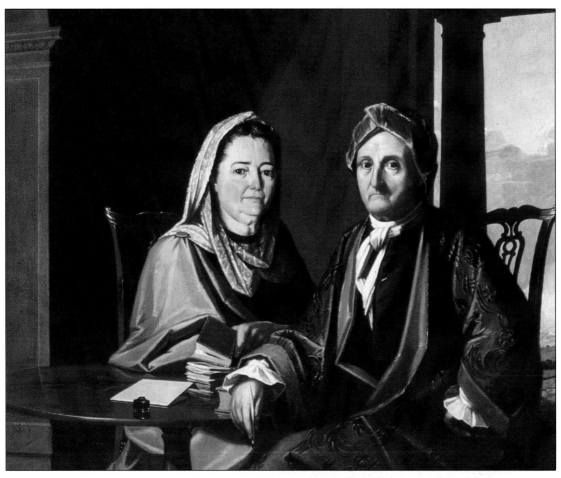

Jonathan and Faith Trumbull, *by John Trumbull, 1778*

became an artist after serving as a soldier in the Revolution. John's celebrated historical paintings include *Battle of Bunker's Hill* and *Capture of the Hessians at Trenton*. George Washington sat for him several times.

Legislative. The lawmaking branch of state government has two houses, the senate and the house of representatives. As of 1995, the senate had 36 members, and there were 151 people

WOMAN IN THE STATEHOUSE: ELLA GRASSO

State politics have provided some firsts through the years, as in 1974: Ella Tambussi Grasso became the first woman to be elected governor of a state without being preceded in office by her husband. She was also the first Connecticut governor of Italian descent.

Born in Windsor Locks in 1919, Grasso was the daughter of immigrants. Her father, Giacomo, was a baker. She was an excellent student and received a scholarship to attend Mount Holyoke College in Massachusetts. After marrying Thomas Grasso in 1942, she gave birth to a son and a daughter.

Grasso began her public service career at age thirty-three when she was elected state representative. She then served for twelve years as secretary of the state and for four years in the U.S. Congress before running her winning campaign for governor in 1974.

During that same election, voters approved an amendment to the state's 1965 constitution, making it illegal to discriminate on the basis of gender. The women's movement had worked hard to end

discrimination in many areas of American life. Of that movement, Grasso said, "It's done a great deal in a short time to provide equal opportunity for women, and I feel I've been a beneficiary."

On December 31, 1980, Governor Grasso resigned for health reasons. She died of cancer the following year.

in the house, all elected by popular vote to two-year terms. A constitutional amendment passed in 1970 states that legislators must meet at least once a year. Either may be called to meet in special sessions by the governor or by a majority of lawmakers in each chamber (house).

State budgets depend on revenues generated by the state income tax and high (6 percent) business and sales taxes. Property taxes are collected by towns for local budgets. Before 1993, Connecticut, unlike most other states, did not have a state income tax. The tax was introduced by Governor Lowell Weicker, and many citizens bitterly opposed it.

A former Republican who had served as a U.S. senator, Weicker won election to the statehouse in 1990 as an Independent. Facing a major shortage in the state budget, Weicker asked the legislature to pass the tax. *Time* magazine called Weicker the "Gutsiest Governor in America." He was also honored with the 1992 Profile in Courage Award, given each year by the President John F. Kennedy Library.

Judicial. The state constitution describes the functions of various state courts and gives the legislature the power to create lower courts. The Connecticut Supreme Court has a chief justice and five full-time associate justices. They hear cases brought by people who believe that their constitutional rights have been violated. The six-judge appellate court may hear cases on appeal (when the parties involved do not agree with the verdict, or decision) from lower courts.

The major trial court for both adult and juvenile cases is a superior court, which has 121 full-time judges. These judges are

Lowell Weicker, seen here in 1987 when he was a U.S. senator from Connecticut, was elected governor in 1988.

first nominated by the governor, then appointed by the General Assembly. They serve eight-year terms. The superior court resolves civil (noncriminal) cases between individuals, as well as the criminal cases that the state brings against individuals.

The state has been governed by a constitution since 1639. New constitutions were written in 1818 and in 1965. The latter has been amended regularly. One amendment, for example, lowered the voting age to eighteen. Another banned discrimination on the basis of sex and mental or physical disability, as well as race, religion, and national origin.

LOCAL GOVERNMENT

A form of government based on town meetings arose throughout colonial New England. In the 1600s and 1700s, Connecticut residents were expected to attend town meetings several times a year. A drummer moved about to announce them. At these meetings, people discussed local matters such as fire protection, a serious concern in those days, and fencing to keep animals out of other people's fields.

Today, under the town government system, people elect their main officials, called selectmen (who can be men or women). Meetings, usually open to the public, can spark lively debates about zoning issues, parking problems, or whether to build a new playground.

Large cities in Connecticut, including Bridgeport, Hartford, New

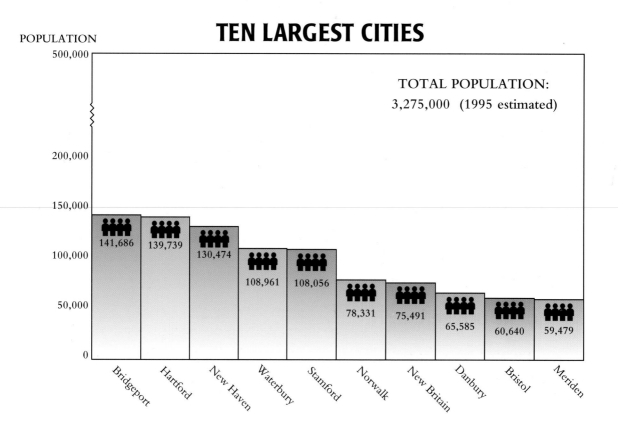

TEN LARGEST CITIES

POPULATION

TOTAL POPULATION:
3,275,000 (1995 estimated)

500,000

200,000

150,000

141,686   139,739

130,474

108,961   108,056

100,000

78,331   75,491

65,585   60,640   59,479

50,000

0

Bridgeport   Hartford   New Haven   Waterbury   Stamford   Norwalk   New Britain   Danbury   Bristol   Meriden

Haven, and Stamford, elect mayors and city councils to run their governments. In 1981, Thirman Milner was elected mayor of Hartford, thereby becoming the first African-American mayor of a New England city. Milner's great-great-great-great-grandfather served in the Revolutionary War.

Citizens can take an active role in politics through the referendum process. An election is held after a certain number of registered voters sign a petition. In 1996, some voters in Westport thought the school budget was too high, so they forced the issue to a vote. Their referendum, asking for cuts in the budget, was then defeated. One man who voted for the referendum said, "Even though we lost this time, it's important that citizens have a chance to say yes or no on these kinds of decisions."

MEETING SOCIAL NEEDS

Poverty and unemployment, especially among minorities, have long concerned citizens and political leaders. During the 1950s and 1960s, the civil rights movement swept across America. People worked to end discriminatory practices in jobs, housing, and schools throughout Connecticut.

In 1957, a group of black ministers joined forces with the National Association for the Advancement of Colored People (NAACP) to elect more African Americans to public office in Connecticut. African Americans became more numerous in politics and law enforcement, on welfare boards, and in school administration.

Inequities in the education system have also received attention. Since the early 1900s, public schools in Connecticut have been under local control, with young people being assigned to schools in their communities. These local school systems raise taxes to fund education, while the state sends additional money to schools on the basis of need.

The state's poorer citizens tend to live in its cities, so urban schools have a disproportionate number of minority and lower-income students. These areas have poorer tax bases, which provide less money for schools. The unequal funding has meant that students in wealthy suburban schools have more modern textbooks

The loss of industrial jobs has left big cities such as Bridgeport with large pockets of poverty and less money to provide good schools and other services.

Hartford student Milo Sheff at a press conference in 1995. In a much publicized case, he accused the state of denying children an equal education—and won.

and equipment, more choices of courses and activities, and better facilities than students in poor urban schools.

Like many states, Connecticut is seeking solutions. Should the state see that all schools receive equal funding? What about instituting a system known as school choice, in which students receive vouchers they can use to attend any school, either public or private? Should students be transported from local schools to regional ones in order to create more diverse racial mixtures?

In 1989, a group in Hartford, including African-American student Milo Sheff, filed a lawsuit against the state. Their attorneys claimed that racial segregation in Connecticut's schools denied all children a quality education. They pointed out that the state constitution promised all children an equal education.

The state supreme court heard the case known as *Sheff v. O'Neill* in 1996. The court ruled in Sheff's favor and directed the state legislature to develop a remedy for the situation. How the state will meet the challenge remains to be seen.

COPING WITH CRIME

Crime has became a major concern across the nation in recent decades. Connecticut has joined other states in setting longer prison terms with less chance for parole. Repeat offenders are now subject to harsher penalties under the state's "persistent offender" laws. Connecticut also has the death penalty. Six people convicted of murder were on death row as of 1996.

During the 1990s, more police were assigned to patrol urban neighborhoods than ever before. State correctional facilities expanded self-help programs for inmates who sought counseling, education, and job training. Crime rates in the state fell during the mid-1990s.

The crime rate in Connecticut varies dramatically from place to place. In some small towns, a murder may occur only once in ten years, if that often. However, in the city of Bridgeport the crime rate is more than four times the national average.

"It's bad here in the projects," says a thirty-four-year-old single mother of two who moved to Bridgeport after emigrating from Brazil to New York City. "The drugs are everywhere. The streets aren't safe for me or my kids." She works at two jobs, in a large grocery store and as a cleaning woman, to make ends meet. With the help of volunteers at a free literacy program in her city, she has improved her English and reading skills.

An extended family of Cambodians who moved to Bridgeport in 1987 recently left that neighborhood. Through a variety of jobs, the family saved enough money to buy a ranch-style home in the smaller, quieter town of Milford. The three teenagers in the family have worked part-time while attending school and college. Their father, who Americanized his name to "Sam," says proudly, "We are citizens now, real Americans. We are doing okay."

A CHANGING ECONOMY

Like immigrants who came before them, these new Americans, many from Asia and Central and South America, have made their way in Connecticut, finding work and a place to live.

New immigrants often take unskilled industrial jobs. Many improve their lives and see their children go on to college and successful careers. Describing the upward mobility that many families experience, a forty-seven-year-old man from the New Haven area says, "My grandfather worked as a mason for this building company when he came to America from Italy. Now, my brothers and I, we own it."

Although the state's economy has changed through the years, manufacturing remains the top industry. Farms, on the decline since 1800, number only about four thousand today. They produce eggs and dairy products and raise chickens, beef cattle, vegetables and

A potbelly pig, wearing a colorful neckerchief, takes a break from a fair in Brooklyn, Connecticut.

fruits, hay, and tobacco. Some farmers have been successful growing flowers and shrubs for nurseries. Tobacco growers, including the Topper Cigar Company in Meriden, benefited from rapidly rising cigar sales during the mid-1990s. The Toppers' family business opened in 1896. A century later, owner Frank Topper said of the boom, "We have a quarter- to a half-million cigars on back order."

As for fishing, harbor and stream pollution limit oyster gathering to Long Island Sound, with only about forty-one thousand acres of oyster beds off the coast. There are also some hard-shell clams,

EARNING A LIVING

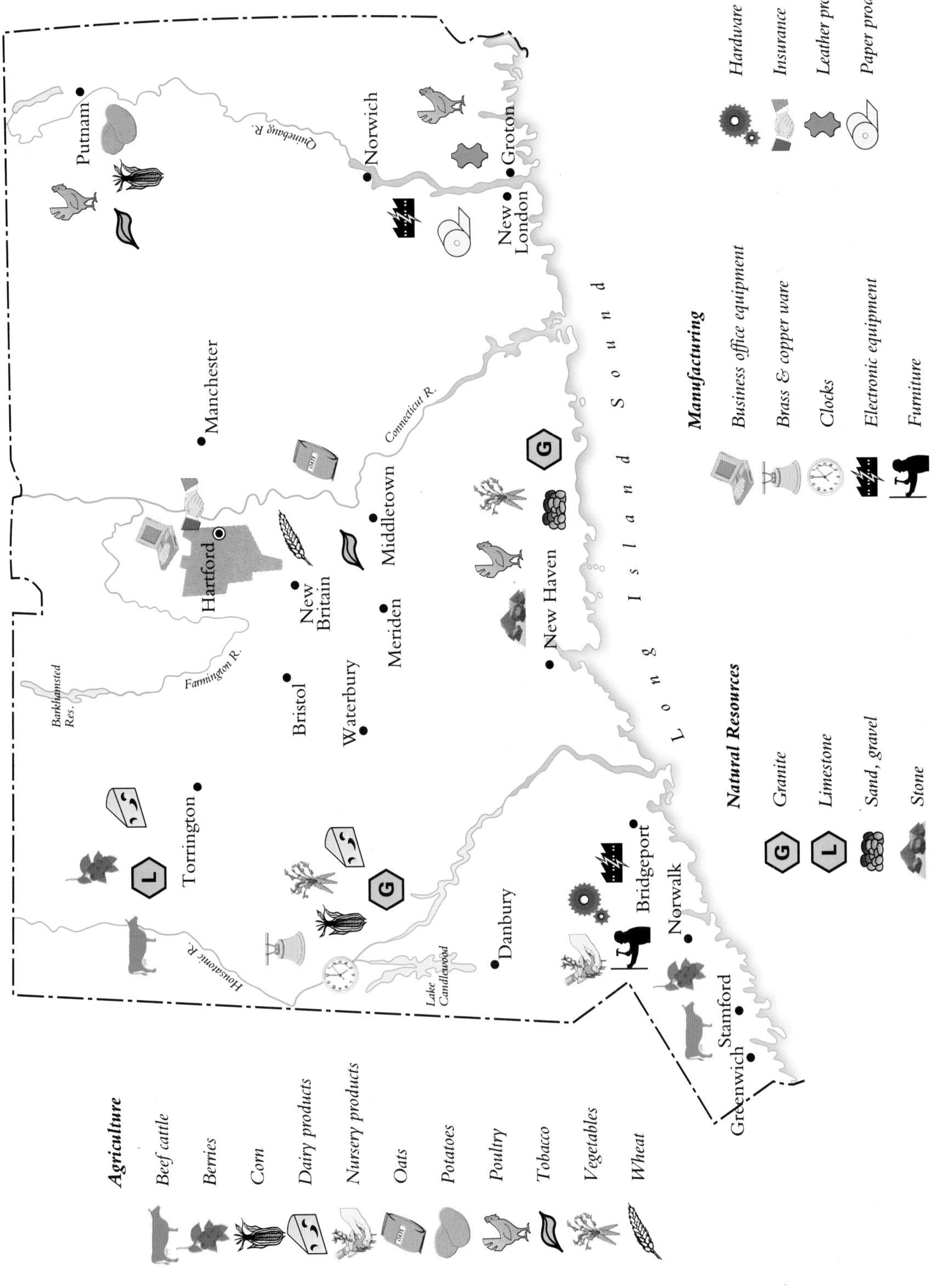

Agriculture
- Beef cattle
- Berries
- Corn
- Dairy products
- Nursery products
- Oats
- Potatoes
- Poultry
- Tobacco
- Vegetables
- Wheat

Manufacturing
- Business office equipment
- Brass & copper ware
- Clocks
- Electronic equipment
- Furniture
- Hardware
- Insurance
- Leather products
- Paper products

Natural Resources
- Granite
- Limestone
- Sand, gravel
- Stone

Putnam

Norwich

Groton

New London

Manchester

Middletown

Hartford

New Britain

Meriden

Bristol

Waterbury

New Haven

Torrington

Danbury

Bridgeport

Norwalk

Stamford

Greenwich

Quinebaug R.

Connecticut R.

Farmington R.

Housatonic R.

Barkhamsted Res.

Lake Candlewood

Long Island Sound

as well as flounder, cod, and lobster. Commercial fishermen in Connecticut catch about thirty-six hundred tons of seafood annually, making this a small part of the state's economy.

With relatively few natural resources, Connecticut continues to rely on manufacturing for jobs. Inventors and innovative thinkers, skilled business managers, skilled and unskilled workers—these are the keystones as the state continues to develop its service and manufacturing industries.

Hartford has been an important center of America's insurance industry since the late 1700s, when sea captains decided to pool sums of money to offset their losses if a ship was wrecked or lost. The first official insurance firm, the Hartford Fire Insurance Company, was organized in 1810. New types of insurance companies sell life, accident, and casualty policies. By the 1990s, thousands of employees worked at about three dozen Hartford-based firms.

1992 GROSS STATE PRODUCT: $82.5 MILLION

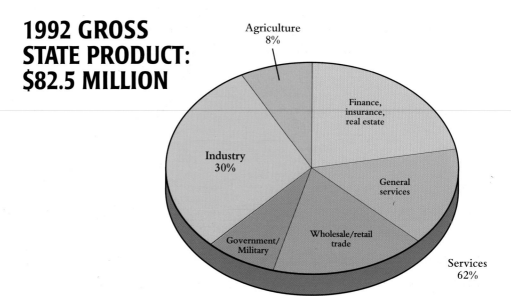

Agriculture
8%

Finance,
insurance,
real estate

Industry
30%

General
services

Government/
Military

Wholesale/retail
trade

Services
62%

*Trident submarines are under construction at the General Dynamics
Corporation in Groton, the submarine capital of the nation.*

For more than forty years, the United States and the communist-governed Soviet Union were engaged in a cold war. Both sides maintained strong military forces and weapons, including nuclear warheads, offensive and defensive missiles, and submarines. The Reagan administration increased military spending during the 1980s. Connecticut businesses and factories received billions of dollars in government contracts. The fall of communism in Eastern Europe brought an end to the cold war and the trimming of America's

Skilled workers put together an airplane engine at Pratt and Whitney in Hartford.

defense arsenal. The state lost more than two hundred thousand jobs between 1989 and 1995.

In Groton, the submarine capital of the world, General Dynamics Electric Boat Division laid off thousands of workers. It lost large defense contracts, which had once provided about half the jobs in that region. Some people left the state to work elsewhere.

One of these unemployed workers was a man in his forties who was employed by General Dynamics for twenty years. Unable to find another job, he took over the jobs of housekeeping and child rearing. His wife, a teacher, returned to her profession. He says, "I've enjoyed being home, being a big part of my kids' lives. They are great, all on the honor roll. [But] I miss the people at my job. The kind of work I did, with machines, you have to keep up your skills. You can't be gone for months, then go back and be in top form."

Submarines, silverware, chemicals, jet engines, processed foods, paint, furniture, helicopters, firearms, ball bearings, cutlery, hand tools, optical instruments, electrical machinery, metalworks—Connecticut's products have run the gamut. As times change, the state must find new goods and services that will bring a healthy economy and sustain the three million people who call Connecticut home.

4 LIVING IN THE NUTMEG STATE

Essex, Connecticut

In March 1996, during a shopping trip in Norwalk, a Connecticut homemaker saw a movie star, a best-selling author, a television journalist, a former congressman, a tree farmer whose family has lived in the state since the 1700s, her fourth-grade son's teacher, a woman from India wearing a sari, and others speaking Spanish, French, and Japanese. People of all kinds, from all places and walks of life—that is Connecticut today. "Your neighbors could be anybody, a retired schoolteacher or Arthur Miller [the famous author]," says Ethyle Power, a resident of Roxbury since 1954.

CELEBRATING DIFFERENCE

After the European colonists, no large wave of immigrants came to the state until the late 1800s. Connecticut has gradually grown more diverse, but the state is still 90 percent white. The 1960 census showed fewer than one thousand Native Americans and about 110,000 African Americans.

The mid-1980s brought a wave of immigration that would bring many new residents to Connecticut. From 1990 to 1995, 36,963 people immigrated to the state from around the world. At the same time, its population fell by several thousand as people laid off from the defense industry moved out of state to look for new jobs.

The state's newest immigrants came from Asia, Africa, South

Children display colorful scarecrows at a contest in Scotland, Connecticut.

America, and Eastern Europe. Most of the Asians emigrated from Cambodia, Laos, Vietnam, Thailand, and Korea. A number of Asian students attend the University of Connecticut in Storrs. It has opened a center for cultural displays and performances and social events where people can enjoy Asian art, music, and literature. Corporations frequently call the school to ask for experts who can teach them how to conduct business in the Far East.

Hungarians make up the largest group from Eastern Europe.

ETHNIC CONNECTICUT

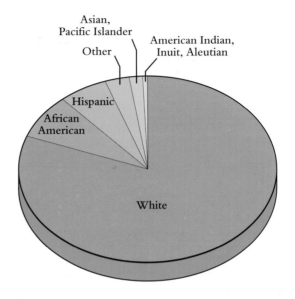

Asian, Pacific Islander

Other

American Indian, Inuit, Aleutian

Hispanic

African American

White

Many live in Fairfield, Stratford, and Bridgeport. The number of Hungarian Americans in Bridgeport and its suburbs is second only to Cleveland, Ohio. Some arrived after the Soviet Union invaded Hungary after World War II and crushed an anti-Soviet rebellion in 1956. Others immigrated after 1989 to escape the crime and unemployment that rose when Soviet domination ended.

TWO CONNECTICUTS

The per capita income of Connecticut—about twenty-nine thousand dollars a year—is the highest in the nation. Average incomes in some communities are forty thousand dollars or more, and an average three- or four-bedroom home may cost several hundred thousand dollars. In cities like Bridgeport, New Haven, and Hartford, incomes are much lower and crime rates and unemployment are higher. That is why some observers say that there are two Connecticuts.

There are often strong contrasts between the lifestyles of people in small towns and those in cities. The gold coast—Greenwich and other wealthy towns along Long Island Sound—is the location of spacious homes, some of them large estates with servants, set on landscaped grounds. There are golf courses, tennis and hunt clubs, polo and croquet games, and marinas filled with yachts and sail-

A view of a privately owned island off Connecticut's gold coast.

boats. Stage, screen, and television personalities mingle with writers, artists, athletes, business executives, and publishers. Some affluent residents use their gold coast homes, which may cost millions of dollars, only as summer or weekend retreats.

Numerous celebrities buy homes in the quiet, northwest part of the state, called Litchfield Hills, as private retreats from New York City or Los Angeles. Steeped in New England tradition, this region features old churches and village greens, colonial and Victorian buildings, and wooded areas.

Most of the communities in Connecticut are classified as towns, many with populations of about twenty thousand or less. Larger cities are far more crowded. Suburban areas near large cities may house upper- or middle-class citizens, while the inner cities are plagued with run-down dwellings and housing projects. Many families live far below the poverty line here. The rates of childhood poverty in Bridgeport, Hartford, and New Haven are among the highest in the nation, a source of ongoing concern to many people in the state.

RELIGIOUS BELIEFS

Since its beginning as a state led by Puritan-Congregationalist clergymen, Connecticut has gradually become more open to other beliefs. In 1818, a new constitution struck down the law that forced everyone to pay taxes to the Congregationalist Church. The church no longer held political control in the state.

Despite the strong Congregational influence, people of other faiths arrived during the colonial period. Jewish citizens have lived

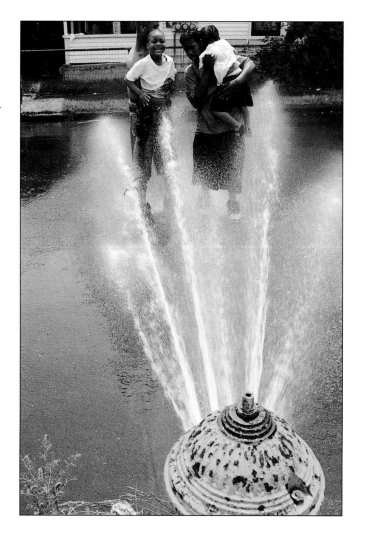

For residents of Bridgeport, water from a fire hydrant offers relief during a summer heat wave.

in Connecticut since the Revolutionary War. Scandinavian and German immigrants brought their diverse Protestant traditions.

In the nineteenth century, Irish Catholic immigrants faced discrimination because of their nationality and religion. Anti-Catholic demonstrations and riots took place around the country. In Hartford, a Catholic church was burned down. Irish citizens worked for acceptance and political change. Some became community leaders. Anti-Catholic sentiments declined, making life

This colonial meetinghouse is located in the town of Washington, which is known for its scenery and country estates.

easier for the Italian and Polish Catholic immigrants who came later.

By the 1990s, Catholics had become the largest single religious group in the state. However, there were more Protestants overall, including Congregationalists, Episcopalians, Lutherans, Presbyterians, Baptists, Methodists, and Quakers. Asian communities included Christians and Buddhists, Hindus, and Shintos. Muslims could also be found throughout Connecticut.

RICH TRADITIONS

People from different cultures have contributed their talents and traditions to life in the state. During one July in 1995, people in southeastern Connecticut could hear an Irish rock group called Big Geraniums, a Baroque concert, Handel's *Water Music*, Hungarian folk singers, show tunes at an outdoor pavilion, Brazilian samba music, or a jazz quartet.

Connecticut's Salt and Pepper Gospel Singers is a group of more than fifty-five people, white and black. They perform at least fifty concerts a year throughout the state at churches, homeless shelters, community events, and prisons.

In Connecticut, national holidays are often marked by traditional New England ceremonies and costumes, some with fifes and drums. Towns may re-create events from their history, such as Revolutionary War battles, on the Fourth of July.

Ethnic restaurants can be found around the state, and people share favorite dishes at food festivals. To the traditional New England cornbreads, baked beans, and meats, new dishes have

SUCCOTASH FOR SUPPER

Traditional dishes in Connecticut were simple and made use of things that were grown at home or on nearby farms. Cooking was plain but hearty and nourishing. During the early days, corn was the main crop, eaten on the cob, in soups, and in various kinds of bread.

Succotash, a favorite dish for supper, used both green corn and beans, especially limas. This tasty version can be made with just a few ingredients:

Creamy Succotash (serves 4-6 people)

2 cups of fresh or frozen lima beans

2½ cups of yellow corn kernels

3 tablespoons butter

1 teaspoon sugar

¼ teaspoon salt

¼ teaspoon pepper, if desired

¾ cup heavy cream

(Ask an adult to help you with this.)

1. Cook the beans, covered with boiling salted water, in a saucepan for seven to eight minutes. They should be tender but still firm.

2. Add the corn and cook for five more minutes. Drain the corn and beans and set aside.

3. Melt the butter in a heavy skillet over medium heat. Add the drained corn and beans and stir to coat. Add the other ingredients and stir until they are well blended.

Succotash goes well with sliced tomatoes, biscuits, and baked apples sweetened with maple syrup.

been added: Irish, Italian, Mexican, Chinese, Japanese, Thai, Hungarian, Bulgarian, Brazilian, Portuguese, Jamaican, and Puerto Rican.

In 1996, Judy Sulik of Bridgeport was so impressed by the many kinds of restaurants in her city that she wrote a restaurant guide and cookbook featuring tasty dishes from these places. A newspaper writer called it "a virtual United Nations of cuisines."

YEAR-ROUND FUN

There is no state fair in Connecticut, but regional fairs, festivals, and cultural events abound. There are art shows, street fairs, flea markets, sailing contests, international food fairs, and many others. Every July, Westport (located on Long Island Sound) sponsors its Great Race, which dates back to the late 1800s. Prizes go to the most unusual and elaborate vessels that can move across the water. Another well-attended boat race is held at Mystic Seaport.

Italians make up the largest ethnic group in the state, and summer is a time for Festival Italiano in many towns. The Sons of Italy sponsor these events to raise money for charities. One fifteen-year-old has gone to the local festival with her family for twelve years and now likes to help her father operate one of the pizza booths. She says, "It's a fun part of summer I just wouldn't miss."

The state is a center for equestrian sports and boasts several well-known hunt and riding clubs. Horse shows draw riders from around the nation. Several Olympic equestrians, including Leslie Burr Howard of Westport, learned their sport while growing up in Connecticut.

The sheep-judging event at the Woodstock Fair gives proud owners a chance to show off their animals.

Snowmobiling, sledding, and downhill and cross-country skiing are favorite winter sports. Connecticut also has a National Hockey League team, the Hartford Whalers. People who moved to Connecticut from other countries have boosted the sport of soccer throughout the state. Jai alai also gained more fans as Latin Americans moved to Connecticut. People from the West Indies have formed cricket teams.

In 1995, the state hosted the Special Olympic Games in New Haven. The largest such games ever, they drew 7,000 athletes, 2,000 coaches, 45,000 volunteers, and more than 500,000 spectators. A number of the Olympians were natives of Connecticut. They included Kathy Ledwidge of Mystic, who has won medals in basketball, soccer, and volleyball, and Kim Musitano of Darien, who has won medals in tennis, bowling, and cross-country skiing.

NEW HORIZONS FOR NATIVE AMERICANS

Several thousand Native Americans live in Connecticut today, both on and off reservations. One tiny reservation, about half a

An athlete paddles to win Manchester's Hockanum River Canoe Race, one of many boat races held in the state each year.

At a Connecticut powwow, deerskin paintings are on display . . .

. . . and both spectators and participants delight in the Girls' Fancy Dance.

block in size, is located in Trumbull. A few Indians also live on the Schagticoke Reservation in Kent. Two large Pequot reservations were set up in Ledyard Town and in North Stonington.

Like other tribes in the United States, the Ledyard group has sovereign status and can operate outside state law. In 1993, the Mashuntucket Pequots created a large gambling-casino complex called Foxwoods. They agreed to pay the state one-fourth of the annual profits from their slot-machine business. The state uses this money to fund social and educational programs in large cities. Foxwoods includes a large gambling building, two hotels, restaurants, shops, three theaters, and a fifteen-hundred-seat showroom for live entertainment. By 1995, Foxwoods was the largest gaming resort in the Western Hemisphere, taking in about one billion dollars a year.

About 1,150 Mohegans live around present-day Norwich and Montville near Fort Shantok State Park. They are one of the largest tribes on the East Coast. Among their members is Gladys Tantaquidgeon, a ninety-six-year-old medicine woman. Indian historian Virginia DeMarce says the tribe survived by learning to adapt: "They shrewdly learned to cope with the new circumstances." In 1996, the Mohegans began building their own large gambling complex. The vast Mohegan Sun Casino includes gaming rooms, restaurants, and a ten-thousand-square-foot nightclub.

The Connecticut Yankees of today may be natives of the state or come from somewhere else in the United States or around the globe. While they share their talents and ideas, they come to know the state's traditions and take part in its future.

5 CONNECTICUT FIRSTS

Revolutionary War reenactment, Coventry

Thanks to Connecticut's dynamic and creative population, the state can boast hundreds of firsts. During its first 150 years, the patent office issued more patents per capita to Connecticut residents than anywhere else. The first patent ever issued to a woman in America was granted to Mary Kies of Connecticut for her machine that wove silk or straw.

Other firsts are: machine to cut the teeth of combs, copper coins, tinware factory, commercial woolen worsted mill, cotton thread factory, hat factory, American-made cigars, steam-powered factory, American plows, hoop skirts, tacks, hook-and-eye fasteners, bicycle factory, condensed milk factory . . . The list goes on and on.

Plus, as proud citizens of the state will tell you, it was not Robert Fulton who built the first steamboat, but John Fitch of Windsor. After moving to Philadelphia, Fitch built three steam-powered boats, and one made regular trips between Philadelphia and Trenton, New Jersey. Another Connecticut man, Samuel Morey, built and ran the first steamboat in the state, making some improvements on Fitch's boat. Fulton, who saw Morey's boat, simply got a patent—and the credit—for the invention.

John Fitch in his first steamboat

A HERO TURNED TRAITOR

Among Connecticut's early figures is a man whose name has gone down in history as a villain. Benedict Arnold, born in Norwich in 1741, joined the Colonial Army in 1775. As captain of the Governor's Foot Guard, he aided in the successful attack on Fort Ticonderoga in New York. A strong patriot, Arnold drew up clever battle plans and showed courage under fire.

Now a general, Arnold received crippling wounds during the Battle of Saratoga in the fall of 1777. While commanding the American forces stationed in Philadelphia, he became friends with Tory families who supported Britain. In 1779, he married a Tory, Margaret (Peggy) Shippen.

By 1780, Arnold, bitter about not receiving a promotion and impoverished from living extravagantly, began spying for the British. He conspired to hand over the American fort at West Point, New York, and then planned a successful attack on Fort Trumbull

In an act of treason, Benedict Arnold persuades John André to hide military papers in his boot.

near New London, Connecticut. In 1781, he led a fierce attack on colonial soldiers at Fort Griswold and burned down the town of New London, enraging the people of Connecticut. Since then, the name Benedict Arnold has meant "traitor."

"MY LIFE FOR MY COUNTRY"

Connecticut may have to claim a traitor as its own, but it can also sing the praises of Revolutionary War hero Nathan Hale. Born in Coventry in 1755, Hale entered Yale College at age fourteen, two years younger than most men of his day. He was a fine scholar, athlete, and orator. After graduating, Hale taught school in East Haddam and then New London.

Hale joined the Continental Army in 1775. The next year, he was made captain of the Knowlton Rangers, a group of 170 much-admired soldiers. He often volunteered for risky assignments. In 1776, Hale went on a special spying mission for General Washington in New York City. There, he gathered information about British battle plans and drew maps showing the sites of their

Revolutionary War hero Nathan Hale is led to his execution.

camps. As he was leaving New York, the British captured Hale.

The twenty-one-year-old former teacher was hanged the next day, September 22, 1776, for spying. Hale's final words appear in most school textbooks and have often been quoted through the years: "I only regret that I have but one life to lose for my country." Hale's courage inspired those who were fighting for liberty.

The schoolhouse where Hale taught in New London was bought in 1902 by the Connecticut Sons of the American Revolution. The group maintains this shingled, one-room school as a monument.

ABOLITIONISTS

Connecticut was home to an active antislavery movement and some famous abolitionists. The first known petition to end slavery in America was written by a Connecticut woman, Hannah Smith. (In later years, her four daughters, also abolitionists, would become famous for refusing to pay taxes until women were allowed to vote.)

Hartford became a center of the antislavery movement and the Underground Railroad, a system of travel routes and hiding places for slaves who escaped from the South. Many slaves were hidden in Connecticut homes on their way to safety in slave-free Canada.

Presbyterian minister Henry Ward Beecher of Litchfield was one of the strongest opponents of slavery. Thousands crowded into Beecher's church every Sunday to hear his eloquent sermons. His sister, Harriet Beecher Stowe, achieved lasting fame with her anti-slavery novel *Uncle Tom's Cabin*, which was published in 1852.

By showing the plight of slaves on Southern plantations, Stowe rallied many Americans to the abolitionist cause. It is said that

Harriet Beecher Stowe's antislavery novel Uncle Tom's Cabin *was read throughout the world.*

when President Abraham Lincoln met the petite fifty-one-year-old author in 1862, he remarked, "So this is the little lady who made this big war?"

The fiery abolitionist John Brown was born in Torrington. In 1855, at age fifty-five, he decided to devote the rest of his life to ending slavery in the United States. In 1859, Brown led a group of twenty-one slaves and supporters in an unsuccessful attack on the federal armory at Harpers Ferry, Virginia. Ten men were killed,

*John Brown died
in his fight to end
slavery.*

including two of his sons. Brown was arrested and later hanged
for treason. But his dream, an end to slavery, would finally come
to pass a few years later.

THE GREATEST SHOW ON EARTH

One of the most colorful people in Connecticut's history was the
celebrated circus-owner, P. T. (Phineas Taylor) Barnum, born in
Bethel in 1810.

Barnum's first attention-grabbing exhibit was a woman named

Joice Heth. She claimed she was 160 years old and had been the nurse of the infant George Washington. In 1841, Barnum set up his American Museum, exhibiting a bearded lady and other curiosities. He also introduced the public to General Tom Thumb, a midget who stood about two feet tall, and his miniature bride, Lavinia Bump Warren. The couple lived in a tiny house in Bridgeport.

Beginning in 1871, Barnum toured Europe and the United States

P. T. Barnum's world-famous circus was billed "The Greatest Show on Earth."

with his three-ring circus, which later joined with James A. Bailey's circus. Barnum lived in Bridgeport until his death in 1891 and kept his circus there during the winter. He served four terms as a state legislator and helped to bring business and industry to the area and also served as the city's mayor. The Barnum Museum in Bridgeport contains memorabilia of his life and times and celebrates Barnum's remarkable career.

SPREADING THE WORD

Connecticut has produced many notable writers and claims some firsts in the fields of writing and publishing. The oldest newspaper in America with a continuous circulation is the *Hartford Courant*, founded in 1764. The first magazine ever published for young Americans, *The Children's Magazine*, was also published here in 1789. So was *American Cookery*, the first cookbook in America, printed in 1796.

New Haven housed America's first public library, started in 1656. In his will, Theophilus Eaton, the former governor of New Haven Colony, left the town a collection of books that had belonged to his deceased brother, which were thereafter made available for public use. In 1803, the town of Salisbury organized the first tax-supported town library in America. Hartford became the site of the first literary group in America, called the Hartford Connecticut Wits.

Noah Webster was born in West Hartford in 1758. Famous for writing the first standard dictionary of American English, he also created teaching methods. During the 1780s, he wrote a three-

Noah Webster, the "Schoolmaster to America," developed dictionaries, spellers, and readers for young people.

volume work called *A Grammatical Institute of the English Language*. The first part of this work became widely known as "Webster's blue-backed speller." Webster's *American Dictionary of the English Language* was published in 1828. His books sold millions of copies and became standard references in schools and libraries.

Connecticut has a long theatrical tradition. Several famous playhouses are located around the state, and plays have often been "tried out" on Connecticut audiences before moving on to Broadway, in New York City. The Yale University School of Drama is known throughout the world and boasts such famous graduates as actress Meryl Streep.

MARK TWAIN: THE MISSISSIPPI COMES TO HARTFORD

Although he was not born in Connecticut, author Samuel Langhorne Clemens, known as Mark Twain, lived in Hartford from the early 1870s into the 1890s. When he first saw the city, Twain called it a "vision of refreshing green."

There he and his wife, Olivia, raised their three daughters in a large Victorian-style house at 351 Farmington Avenue. The house has been called one-third riverboat, one-third cathedral, and one-third cuckoo clock. Twain had the south facade of the house built to look like a Mississippi River steamboat, complete with decks and a pilot house. He placed the kitchen in the front of the house rather than in the back so that the servants would be able to see "life go by" as they worked. The fanciful Mark Twain House is now a museum open to the public.

Twain wrote some of his most important works while he lived in Hartford, including *The Adventures of Tom Sawyer, The Prince and the Pauper, The Adventures of Huckleberry Finn*, and *A Connecticut Yankee in King Arthur's Court*.

During the 1890s and early 1900s, the family lived in Europe. In 1908, Twain moved to a home in Redding, Connecticut, where he died in 1910.

Among the playwrights with a Connecticut connection is Eugene O'Neill, whom some critics regard as America's finest. Born in New York City, O'Neill was a newspaper reporter in New London, Connecticut, where his father, a famous actor, lived. The O'Neill home, and a nearby lighthouse with its foghorn, provided the setting for O'Neill's most famous play, *Long Day's Journey into Night*. His one comedy, *Ah, Wilderness!* (1933), was also set in Connecticut. In 1936, O'Neill won the Nobel Prize for literature.

AN ADVOCATE FOR THE DEAF

Philadelphia native Thomas Hopkins Gallaudet graduated from Yale College, then became a leading teacher and advocate for the deaf. After seeing Gallaudet's successful efforts to teach a girl who had lost her hearing at age two, prominent citizens in Hartford raised more than two thousand dollars to found a free school for the deaf, the first of its kind in the Western Hemisphere. Gallaudet studied teaching methods in England and France, then returned to set up the school. It received additional funding from the Connecticut General Assembly; this was the first time a state had provided funds to aid handicapped citizens. Gallaudet College (now called Gallaudet University) in Washington, D.C., was named in his honor, and his son became its first president.

ART AND MUSIC

Many composers, including Richard Rodgers of the famous song-writing team Rodgers and Hammerstein, have owned homes in

Connecticut. Danbury native Charles Ives, born in 1874, started out as an insurance-company executive, then became a composer. A pioneer of modern musical composition, Ives experimented with unusual rhythms and combinations of notes. He won the Pulitzer Prize for music in 1947 and was nicknamed the Walt Whitman of American Music, a comparison to the well-known poet.

Thanks to a Connecticut inventor, since 1948 recorded music could be heard more clearly than ever before. Peter Carl Goldmark invented the first long-playing (LP) "33⅓" record. Earlier records, called 78s because they revolved around the turntable seventy-eight times per minute, were made of heavy shellac that was breakable. These thick 78s took eight times more shelf space than Goldmark's innovation. His LPs, with their improved sound, were welcomed by people all over the world.

Among the contemporary musicians who own homes in Connecticut are Michael Bolton, Ashford and Simpson, Meatloaf, and Jose Feliciano.

Connecticut has given the world several notable artists. One of the most remarkable is Norwich native Elis Ruley, who was completely self-taught. Ruley did not start painting until 1929, when he was forty-seven years old. He had been hit by a truck and was too disabled to return to his former job. Sitting at home, he felt a desire to paint and began experimenting with different materials.

Ruley painted the scenes and people around him, giving a unique view of small-town Connecticut and African-American life. Many of his works were done with house paint on poster board. In 1996, sixty of Ruley's paintings were featured at a special exhibit held at the Wadsworth Atheneum, a museum in Hartford.

SPORTSWOMEN

Some of America's top women athletes have come from Connecticut. Since 1947, the town of Stratford has hosted the most famous women's softball team in the world—the Raybestos Brakettes, now called the Stratford Brakettes. In 1965, this team was part of a world tour that promoted women's softball. It represented the United States at the Women's World Fast Pitch Softball tournament in Melbourne, Australia, the same year. The Brakettes began under the sponsorship of the Raybestos Products Company and won twenty-three national titles and three world titles in its first fifty years. In the early 1970s, the team won five straight national championships, led by its famous pitcher and first baseman, Joan Joyce.

Joan Joyce prepares to pitch at the 1974 World Women's Softball Championship, where the U.S. team won its first world title.

In 1996, the Raybestos Company moved to Indiana, and the team had to find a new sponsor or break up. Bob Wirz, head of a sports public-relations and marketing company in Milford, Connecticut, was among those who worked to keep the team going. Said Wirz, "I knew about the team's tradition and realized that the Brakettes were a state treasure."

Other sports headliners included Rebecca Lobo, a star on the

Rebecca Lobo gets off a jump shot at the NCAA East Regional Championship at Storrs, Connecticut, in March 1995.

women's basketball team at the University of Connecticut. In 1994–1995, the team went undefeated and won the national collegiate title. Lobo was named best female college basketball player in the nation. She played as a member of the U.S. women's team that won the gold medal in basketball at the 1996 Olympic Games in Atlanta, Georgia.

One of the most popular women athletes of all time was figure skater Dorothy Hamill, who was born in Riverside, Connecticut, in 1956. Hamill blended artistry with dazzling athletic jumps and spins on the ice.

In both 1974 and 1975, Hamill won the U.S. women's national title. She was disappointed when she fell while competing at the 1975 world championships. A year later, at the Olympic Games in Innsbruck, Austria, Hamill won the gold medal for women's figure skating. She skated a clean and difficult program, winning all three phases of the competition—required figures, short program, and long free-skating program. Her bright smile endeared her to spectators, and her short "wedge" hairdo sparked a national fad. After the Olympics, Hamill became a professional skater with the Ice Capades and competed in many pro skating events.

A FILM LEGEND TURNS PHILANTHROPIST

Actor Paul Newman often received compliments for the salad dressing he created in the kitchen of his Connecticut country home, shared with his actress-wife Joanne Woodward and their children. Friends urged Newman to market the dressing. This business venture only began to appeal to him when he realized that all the profits could go to charity.

Paul Newman shows reporters his Hole-in-the-Wall-Gang Camp for children with serious illnesses shortly before it opens.

Under the label Newman's Own, the company began to sell salad dressing, then spaghetti sauce, popcorn, salsa, and lemonade. Sales of Newman's Own were so successful that the company was able to build and operate its Hole-in-the-Wall-Gang Camp, a special retreat in Connecticut for children with cancer and other serious illnesses. The camp took its name from one of Newman's popular films, *Butch Cassidy and the Sundance Kid*.

Newman's Own has contributed millions of dollars a year to other charitable causes. Money is given to schools, community organizations, educational groups, homeless shelters, and environmental groups, among others.

In large ways and small, people in Connecticut reach out to their neighbors and the larger community. They carry on a tradition that began back in colonial days when communities joined together to clear stumps from a field or raise a neighbor's barn.

6 PLACES TO SEE, THINGS TO DO

Because of Connecticut's compact size, a person can cross it in two or three hours, moving from quiet, traditional villages to bustling cities, from a ski resort to a seaport, all in the same day. It has also been said that a motorist driving on the highway is never more than thirty minutes away from a state park.

The state's three million people are connected by a broad highway system, including the Connecticut Turnpike and the Merritt Parkway. The curving, tree-lined Merritt is considered one of the most scenic highways in America. Those who prefer trains can commute on more than 610 miles of railroad track, including the Metro North Railroad, which runs between Grand Central Terminal in New York City and New Haven, with stops in between.

The train is also a convenient way to get to plays, concerts, or sports events. Young people ride into New York City to see baseball, hockey, and tennis matches, or to attend concerts by favorite musicians. Some young performers who live in southern Connecticut take the train when they have parts in a Broadway play, or to film commercials, many of which are made in New York City.

In recent years, many Connecticut residents have discovered that they can go "on vacation" in their own state: They are enjoying day and weekend trips near home.

Collectible dolls please doll lovers at this antiques fair in Fairfield County.

FAIRFIELD COUNTY AND THE GOLD COAST

At the southwest corner of the state, along Long Island Sound and close to New York City, lies the so-called gold coast, a row of wealthy communities: Greenwich, Darien, Stamford, Norwalk, Westport, Southport, and Fairfield. Mostly residential, these towns feature fine shopping areas and great restaurants of all kinds. During summer or fall, visitors driving along country roads in Fairfield County will find outdoor flea markets, antiques stores, and farm stands selling fruits and vegetables.

The city of Bridgeport contains several museums and landmarks. Downtown, the Discovery Museum features hands-on science exhibits that teach visitors about nuclear energy, electricity, and magnetism. Beardsley Zoological Gardens features typical farm animals along with wild and rare species. There is a re-creation of a tropical rain forest, as well as woodlands, a large lake, and a garden.

Visitors to the P. T. Barnum Museum can trace the great showman's career, learn about the history of circuses, and see pictures of people and businesses in Bridgeport from earlier days.

Many Connecticut towns feature well-designed nature centers. The Audubon Center in Greenwich is well worth a visit. It covers 280 acres of woodlands, with rare tree specimens, and meadows, ponds, and streams. One ten-year-old who visited the center on a school field trip especially liked watching a beehive and birds through an observation window.

NEW HAVEN COUNTY

Moving east along the southern coast of the state, you reach New Haven County. This area is rich in history and has become a center for the arts. The Yale University Art Gallery opened in 1832 and was the first university art museum in the Western Hemisphere. Starting with one hundred paintings, a gift from artist John Trumbull, the museum built a collection of art from around the world. The Yale Center for British Art and British Studies has amassed the largest collection of British art outside the United Kingdom. Also at Yale is the Peabody Museum of Natural History, known for its Native American displays and Great Hall of Dinosaurs.

Visitors can learn about the history of circuses and their famous showmen at the P. T. Barnum Museum in Bridgeport.

On the coast south of New Haven is Branford, which was founded in 1644. Vacationers have long enjoyed visiting Stony Creek, a typical New England fishing village near the town. On boat tours you will hear tales about the pirates who raided ships along the coast centuries ago. The Thimble Islands off Branford are said to hold lost pirate treasure. Even if you don't find buried treasure,

The picturesque rocky shoreline at Stony Creek Thimble

you can fish or sit and watch the gulls, cormorants, and herons find their dinner.

MIDDLESEX COUNTY

To the east of Branford and up the Connecticut River lies Hadlyme, site of a simulated medieval castle that draws some hundred thousand visitors each year. Gillette Castle was the home of William Gillette, a stage actor and playwright of the early 1900s. The fieldstone castle, built between 1914 and 1919, rises from a bluff over a bank of the Connecticut River. The outside is adorned with fairy-castle turrets, arches, and fountains. Its twenty-four rooms contain fancy carvings, fine woodwork, and elegant furniture. Gillette was famous for portraying detective Sherlock Holmes, and he decorated a room in his castle to look like Holmes's London study.

Gillette Castle, perched on a bluff overlooking the Connecticut River, is an impressive sight.

Another interesting building in nearby East Haddam is the Goodspeed Opera House, a Victorian replica of a famous opera house in Paris. The building was restored as a museum, then turned into a theater. Shows were brought there from New York City during the early 1900s by steamer.

A visit to East Haddam is not complete without seeing the bell at St. Stephen's Episcopal Church. It was made A.D. 815 and originally hung in a Spanish monastery. The bell was taken to New York City on a nineteenth-century trading ship, and William Pratt, a ship chandler, shipped it to his hometown of East Haddam. It is thought to be the world's oldest church bell.

THE SUBMARINE CAPITAL

On the coast near the eastern border of Connecticut is the town of Groton. Located here are the U.S. naval submarine base, the naval submarine school, and the USS *Nautilus* Memorial. As you would expect, visitors to Groton can learn about America's maritime history and tour submarines. The amazing and powerful atomic *Nautilus* was used both as a carrier of defense weapons and for underwater exploration thousands of leagues beneath the Arctic ice. Also on display are submarines from the days of the Revolutionary War to the present.

Visitors can actually test seawater and learn how to identify various sea creatures when they climb aboard Project Oceanology. Educational cruises are offered throughout the summer.

At nearby Fort Griswold State Park is a monument to soldiers who were killed during the 1781 massacre by British troops led by

PLACES TO SEE

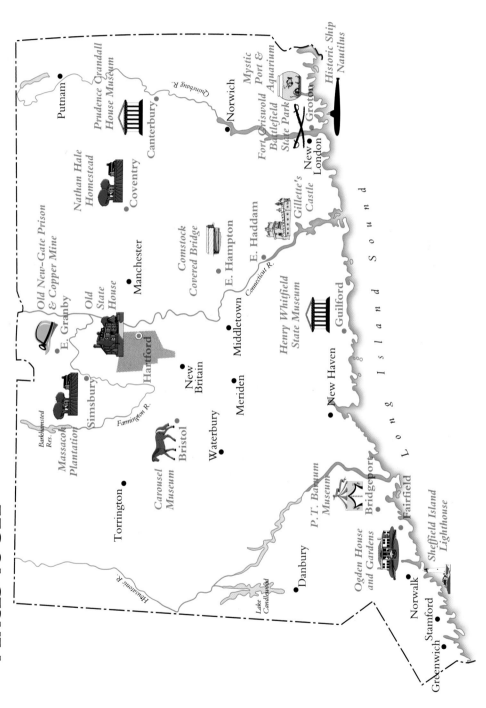

Putnam

Prudence Crandall
House Museum

Quinebaug R.

Canterbury

Norwich

Mystic
Port &
Aquarium

Fort Griswold
Battlefield
State Park

Groton

Historic Ship
Nautilus

New
London

Nathan Hale
Homestead

Coventry

Old New-Gate Prison
& Copper Mine

E. Granby

Old
State
House

Manchester

Comstock
Covered Bridge

E. Hampton

E. Haddam

Gillette's
Castle

Connecticut R.

Hartford

Middletown

Henry Whitfield
State Museum

Guilford

Barkhamsted
Res.

Simsbury

Massacoh
Plantation

Farmington R.

New
Britain

Meriden

Waterbury

Bristol

Carousel
Museum

New Haven

Long Island Sound

Torrington

Housatonic R.

Danbury

Lake
Candlewood

P. T. Barnum
Museum

Bridgeport

Fairfield

Ogden House
and Gardens

Norwalk

Sheffield Island
Lighthouse

Stamford

Greenwich

Benedict Arnold. A museum details the history of that event and also shows the history of the whaling industry.

HARTFORD AND CENTRAL CONNECTICUT

Because the earliest settlements were built in central Connecticut, many historical sites, monuments, old buildings, and museums are found here. Hartford, the state's oldest city and its capital, holds much of interest, both old and new. The oldest free art museum in the country, Wadsworth Atheneum, was built there in 1842. The Connecticut Historical Society Museum is also located in the state capital.

The elegant old statehouse was designed by America's first native-born architect, Charles Bulfinch. Built in 1796, it is the oldest statehouse in the United States and is listed as a national landmark. This building was erected on the site where the Fundamental Orders were ratified and served as the capitol from 1796 to 1878. Here, too, Washington planned important strategy for the Revolutionary War and his campaign in Yorktown. Connecticut delegates met in it to discuss ratifying the United States Constitution.

Under the direction of Bill Faude, the old statehouse was renovated between 1992 and 1996. A carillon on the roof now plays music and lets off a booming noise when an important event takes place. Like modern Connecticut itself, the building celebrates diversity and blends old and new, with its historical exhibits, Latino artwork, and elegant Great Senate Room. The building is used by people in the community for debates, speeches, weddings, and school functions. Says Faude, "This building is to serve people.

The old statehouse in Hartford was the scene of important political events in our nation's past.

This is not a museum for . . . pewter spoons."

The present capitol opened in 1878 and the first General Assembly met there the next year. This newer building is fashioned of Connecticut marble, with statues and medallions on the outside showing important people and events in the state's history. Objects of interest inside are the camp bed used by French general Lafayette during the Revolutionary War and a figurehead from the ship *Hartford*, which was commanded by Admiral David

Farragut, a leading naval commander for the Union Army during the Civil War.

Summer visitors who love flowers will relish the stunning Elizabeth Park Rose Gardens. This park, with fifteen thousand rose bushes of more than eight hundred kinds, was the first municipal rose garden in the United States. Other areas of the park hold rock gardens and beds of flowers, plants, and herbs.

Southeast of Hartford, Bristol contains the fascinating New England Carousel Museum. A unique display of carousel-related items shows the kinds of rides children enjoyed in amusement parks around 1900. Some of the horses and other figures are fine works of art, carefully carved and painted with precise details. A workshop shows visitors how carousel figures are made.

HILLS AND VILLAGE GREENS

The steep, picturesque hills and quaint villages of northern Connecticut attract many tourists, including artists. One charming feature still present in many old towns is the village green, also called a "common" because these acres of open land in the center of town were owned in common by all the citizens. Outdoor community activities—meetings, military drills, and public hangings—took place there. Some were used for grazing cows. Today, they may hold concerts or art fairs.

The town of Cornwall boasts an old covered bridge that spans the Connecticut River. Many artists have drawn or painted it or have been inspired by the forested hills around the town.

Another town in northern Connecticut, Simsbury, has become

an international figure-skating center. Skaters from around the world, including 1994 Olympic gold medalist Oksana Baiul of the Ukraine, now live in Simsbury and train at this rink. Ice shows attract visitors from around the country.

Of course there is much more to do in Connecticut: There is hiking, boating, fishing, camping, swimming, skiing in the mountains of the north. There are restored colonial and Indian villages, dozens of art and science museums, homes where famous people once lived and worked, and car, boat, and balloon races. There are miles of winding rivers and state parks to explore. In that small but vigorous state called Connecticut, there are enough possible adventures to fill several lifetimes.

Hot-air balloons soar above Bristol.

THE FLAG: The flag shows the state coat of arms on a field of azure. Below is a streamer that bears the state motto in blue letters. The state flag was adopted in 1897.

THE SEAL: The state seal is in the form of an ellipse. Around the outer border are the Latin words "Sigillum Reipublicae Connecticutensis," which mean Seal of the Republic of Connecticut. In the center of the ellipse, three staked grapevines form a "V." The grapevines symbolize the culture of the Old World (Europe) being transplanted to the New World. Below the grapevine is a streamer with the state motto. The seal was adopted in 1931.

STATE SURVEY

Statehood: January 9, 1788

Origin of Name: Connecticut comes from an Indian word meaning "beside the long tidal river." The river referred to is the Connecticut River, which divides the state in half from north to south.

Nickname: Constitution State, Nutmeg State, the Land of Steady Habits

Capital: Hartford

Motto: He Who Transplanted Still Sustains

Bird: American robin

Animal: Sperm whale

Insect: Praying mantis

Flower: Mountain laurel

Tree: White oak

Mineral: Garnet

Ship: U.S.S. *Nautilus*

Robin

Mountain laurel

YANKEE DOODLE

During the Revolutionary War, British soldiers sang mocking verses to poke fun at the Americans. American soldier Edward Banks, on hearing one song, decided that he would write new lyrics that the Yankees could sing back at the British. It is this version of "Yankee Doodle" that has gone down in American history and become Connecticut's unofficial state song.

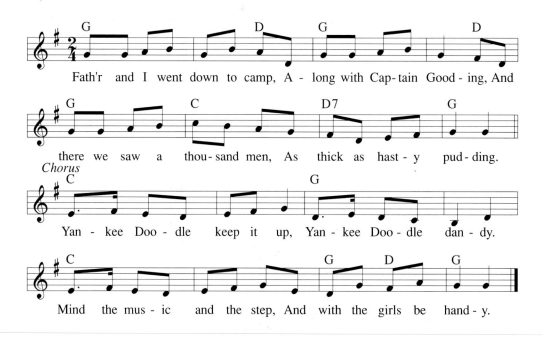

And there we see a thousand men
As rich as Squire David,
And what they wasted every day
I wish it could be saved. *Chorus*

The 'lasses they eat every day
Would keep a house a winter;
They have as much that I'll be bound
They eat it when they're a mind to. *Chorus*

And there we see a swamping gun,
Large as a log of maple,
Upon a deuced little cart,
A load for father's cattle. *Chorus*

And every time they shoot it off,
It takes a horn of powder,
It makes a noise like father's gun,
Only a nation louder. *Chorus*

And Captain Davis had a gun,
He kind of clapped his hand on't,
And stuck a crooked stabbing iron
Upon the little end on't. *Chorus*

I see a little barrel, too,
The heads were made of leather,
They knocked upon with little clubs,
And called the folks together. *Chorus*

And there was Captain Washington,
And gentle folks about him;
They say he's grown so tarnal proud
He will not ride without them. *Chorus*

He got him on his meeting-clothes,
Upon a slapping stallion,
He set the world along in rows,
In hundreds and in millions. *Chorus*

The flaming ribbons in his hat,
They looked so taring fine, ah,
I wanted pockily to get
To give to my Jemimah. *Chorus*

GEOGRAPHY

Highest Point: 2,380 feet above sea level, at Mount Frissell

Lowest Point: Sea level, at Long Island Sound

Area: 5,018 square miles

Greatest Distance, North to South: 75 miles

Greatest Distance, East to West: 90 miles

Bordering States: Massachusetts to the north, Rhode Island to the east, New York to the west

Hottest Recorded Temperature: 105°F at Waterbury on July 22, 1926

Coldest Recorded Temperature: −32°F at Falls Village on February 16, 1943

Average Annual Precipitation: 44 to 48 inches

Major Rivers: Connecticut, Farmington, Housatonic, Mad, Naugatuck, Pequonnock, Pootatuck, Quinnebaug, Salmon, Shepaug, Shetucket, Thames, Weekeepeemee

Major Lakes: Candlewood, Gaillard, Lillinonoah, Mansfield Hollow

Trees: ash, beech, birch, cedar, dogwood, elm, hemlock, hickory, hop hornbeam, horse chestnut, ironwood, maple, oak, pine, sycamore, willow

Wild Plants: bayberry, black raspberry, bloodroot, blueberry, cowslip, hepatica, huckleberry, Indian pipe, jack-in-the-pulpit, juniper berry, lady's slipper, lupine, mountain laurel, pennyroyal, sheep laurel, sweet fern, trailing arbutus, wild cherry

Animals: beaver, cottontail rabbit, fox, mink, muskrat, opossum, otter, raccoon, skunk, squirrel, white-tailed deer, woodchuck

Birds: bluebird, bluejay, bobwhite, cardinal, chickadee, crow, duck, goldfinch, meadowlark, oriole, owl, partridge, quail, ring-necked pheasant, robin, ruffed grouse, sparrow, thrush, warbler, whippoorwill, wild turkey, woodcock, woodpecker

Fish: blackfish, bluefish, bluegill, brook trout, brown trout, bullhead, butterfish, calico bass, cod, flounder, largemouth bass, mackerel, perch, pickerel, pollack, porgy, rainbow trout, shad, smallmouth bass, smelt, sockeye salmon, striped bass, sunfish, swordfish

Endangered Animals: bald eagle, bog turtle, grasshopper, least shrew, long-eared owl, peregrine falcon, red-headed woodpecker, sparrow

Bog turtle

Endangered Plants: balsam fir, bog rosemary, Devil's bit, dwarf mistletoe, goldenseal, hairy lip fern, Indian paintbrush, large-leaved sandwort, panic grass, red mulberry, rough-leaved aster, showy lady's-slipper, side-oats grama-grass, white milkweed

TIMELINE

Connecticut History

1614 Adriaen Block sails up Connecticut River and claims surrounding land for Dutch

1633 Dutch build a fur-trading post at Hartford; the English build their first settlement at Windsor

1637 John Mason and his army defeat Indians in Pequot War

1638 New Haven is founded

1639 Three River Towns of Hartford, Wethersfield, and Windsor unite to form Connecticut Colony. Fundamental Orders of Connecticut adopted by the Connecticut Colony

1662 Connecticut Colony officially chartered

1665 New Haven becomes part of Connecticut Colony

1701 Yale University founded

1740 First tinware in America made by Edward and William Pattison

1775 Revolutionary War begins

1776 Nathan Hale is executed by British as a spy

1781 Benedict Arnold leads British troops in raid on New London

1784 Connecticut Emancipation Law passed; children born to slaves would be free at age 25. America's first law school founded at New Litchfield

1788 Connecticut becomes fifth state

1794 Cotton gin patented by Eli Whitney

1798 Eli Whitney mass produces standard parts for muskets at Whitneyville

1818 New state constitution ratified

1835 Samuel Colt develops six-shooter

1837 First railroad in service in Connecticut

1839 Charles Goodyear discovers vulcanization of rubber

1841 U. S. Supreme Court decides in favor of the Africans who fought for their freedom en route to Cuba aboard the *Amistad*

1844 Horace Wells uses first anesthesia

1845 Elias Howe invents sewing machine

1875 Hartford becomes state's only capital

1882 Knights of Columbus founded at New Haven

1888 Centennial celebration

1898 First car insurance in America issued at Hartford

1917 United States submarine base established at Groton

1954 First atomic submarine, the *Nautilus*, launched at Groton

1965 Present state constitution is adopted

1966 Dinosaur tracks found at Rocky Hill

1974 Ella Grasso elected governor

1983 Major road-building program begun

1984 Ellen Ash Peters becomes first woman named to Connecticut Supreme Court

1991 State's first income tax is passed

ECONOMY

Agricultural Products: apples, eggs, milk and dairy products, potatoes, poultry, strawberries, tobacco

Manufactured Products: airplane engines, boats, brass products, clocks,

Triton

electrical products, foods, helicopters, metal products, rubber products, silverware, submarines

Natural Resources: clay, feldspar, gravel, sand, stone, traprock

Business and Trade: communications, finance, insurance, real estate, transportation, wholesale and retail trade

CALENDAR OF CELEBRATIONS

Silvermine Chamber Music Series From May through September, Westport hosts this series of live theater and music.

Branford Festival The popular vacation spot of Branford celebrates Father's Day each June with this festival on the town green.

Main Street U.S.A. New Britain holds a community festival the second Saturday of June.

Taste of Old Saybrook The local restaurants set up booths along the town's sidewalks during July to give residents and visitors a chance to sample their favorite dishes. Taste everything from rich desserts to ethnic dishes such as Thai.

Old Saybrook's Arts and Crafts Show Artists from all over the state and 25,000 visitors arrive during the last weekend in July to set up booths in this historic town.

Italian Festival This July celebration in New Britain features Italian food, arts, and crafts.

New Haven Jazz Festival Every July, the town green swings to the sound of America's music, jazz.

Midsummer Festival On the first Saturday in August, visitors to the Lyme Academy of Fine Arts can listen to live music, watch painting demonstrations, and buy students' artwork.

Chrysanthemum Festival During this month-long festival that begins in mid-August, Bristol celebrates the arrival of autumn with a display of ethnic foods, cultures, and customs.

Flight of the Beautiful Balloons Every September, colorful hot-air balloons soar high in the sky over Long Island Sound. From the shore, spectators can listen to country and rock music, look at crafts, and enter or watch shipbuilding contests as the balloons sail overhead.

Norwalk Oyster Festival Norwalk celebrates its important oyster industry with a three-day festival in September. Seafood is abundant, with plenty of oysters and clams to eat while enjoying the live entertainment. Kids' Cove features amusement rides, magic tricks, and lots of games.

Southington Apple Harvest Festival The first two weekends in October are set aside for this celebration of the rich tastes and colors of autumn.

Main Street Stroll Old Saybrook hosts this winterfest on the first weekend of December. The highlight of the festival, the torchlight parade, gives participants the chance to walk back into colonial times.

STATE STARS

Dean Gooderham Acheson (1893–1971) was born in Middletown. As a statesman, he advised several American presidents, including Truman,

Kennedy, and Johnson. He served as U.S. undersecretary of state from 1945 to 1947. As secretary of state from 1949 to 1952, he helped draft the Marshall Plan. In 1970 he received the Pulitzer Prize in history for *Present at the Creation*, his book about his service in the State Department.

Dean Acheson

Phineas Taylor (P. T.) Barnum (1810–1891) was America's greatest showman in the nineteenth century. He helped found the Ringling Brothers Barnum and Bailey Circus, "The Greatest Show on Earth." He was born in Bethel.

Paul Wayland Bartlett (1865–1925) was a sculptor born in New Haven. His most famous sculpture was "The Dying Lion." He also executed a famous statue of Lafayette, the French hero of the Revolutionary War, which was given to France as a gift from the children of America.

Hiram Bingham (1875–1956) was a professor of archaeology at Yale when he discovered the Inca ruins at Machu Picchu in 1911. He served as governor of Connecticut in 1925 and then served in the U.S. Senate from 1925 to 1933.

Al Capp (1909–1979) was the creator of the famous comic strip "L'il Abner." He was born in New Haven as Alfred Gabriel Caplin.

Glenn Close (1947–   ) is a successful screen and stage actress who was born in Greenwich. She starred in the hit films *The Big Chill* and *Fatal Attraction* and won a Tony Award for her role in *The Real Thing* in 1984.

Glenn Close

Roger Connor (1857–1931) starred for 18 years in the National League as a first baseman, mostly for the New York Giants. At various times in his career, he led the league in batting, slugging, doubles, triples, home runs, and runs batted in. He was elected to the Baseball Hall of Fame in 1976. He was born in Waterbury.

Charles Goodyear (1800–1860) was an inventor born in New Haven. He discovered that heating, or vulcanizing, rubber would keep it from melting and sticking in hot weather. His invention made rubber practical for a number of new uses, especially for tires.

John Pierpont (J. P.) Morgan (1837–1913) was born in Hartford. He amassed one of America's greatest fortunes. As a financier, he helped organize some of the largest U.S. corporations, such as AT&T, General Electric, International Harvester, and U.S. Steel. He donated paintings, sculptures, and books to many libraries and museums.

Ralph Nader (1934–   ) was born in Winsted. After Nader earned a law degree from Harvard, he became interested in consumer protection. He wrote *Unsafe at Any Speed*, which criticized the automobile industry and pushed for safer cars. The book was a best-seller and led to the passage of the National Traffic and Motor Vehicle Safety Act in 1966. Since then, Nader has influenced several key pieces of legislation. He heads a nonprofit agency, The Public Interest Research Group, known as Nader's Raiders.

Ralph Nader

Frederick Law Olmstead (1822–1903) was a landscape architect born in Hartford. He designed New York City's Central Park and many other park spaces in urban areas across the country.

Eugene O'Neill (1888–1953) spent his boyhood summers in New London. Regarded by many as America's greatest playwright, he won the 1936 Nobel Prize in literature. His greatest play, *Long Day's Journey into Night*, is based on his own family.

Rosa Ponselle (1897–1981) was an operatic soprano born in Meriden. She starred with the New York Metropolitan Opera from 1918 to 1937, appearing in *Don Giovanni, La Giocanda,* and *Aida*.

Roger Sherman (1721–1793) was the only colonial statesman to sign all four of the following documents: the Articles of Association, the Articles of Confederation, the Declaration of Independence, and the Constitution.

Benjamin Silliman (1816–1885) was one of the foremost American scientists of his day. A chemist and toxicologist who did groundbreaking work in the use of petroleum products, he helped found the National Academy of Sciences in 1863. He was born in New Haven and taught for many years at Yale.

Benjamin Spock (1903–   ) is the pediatrician who wrote the best-selling nonfiction book of all time, *Baby and Child Care*. Since it was first published in 1946, millions of American parents have consulted this book for advice on raising their children. Born in New Haven, Spock led

Rosa Ponselle

opposition to United States involvement in the Vietnam War in the 1960s and was a presidential candidate in 1972.

Harriet Beecher Stowe (1811–1896) was born in Litchfield. An abolitionist and author, her most famous book was *Uncle Tom's Cabin*, which was published in 1852. This enormously popular novel portrayed slavery as a morally evil system and helped influence the attitudes that led to the Civil War.

Noah Webster (1758–1843) was born in Hartford. Educated at Yale, Webster became the foremost American expert on the English language. A lexicographer, lawyer, and newspaper publisher, Webster compiled the *Elementary Spelling Book* and *The American Dictionary of the English Language*.

Harriet Beecher Stowe

Elihu Yale (1649–1721) was an English philanthropist who donated books and other valuable items to the Collegiate School of Connecticut. The school was renamed Yale University in his honor.

TOUR THE STATE

Henry C. Bowen House (Woodstock) This Gothic revival house was built in 1846 and is known as Roseland Cottage or the Pink House.

Henry C. Bowen House

Christopher Leffingwell House Museum (Norwich) Officers in the Continental Army, including George Washington, visited this patriot's home during the Revolutionary War. Historical furniture and artifacts from the period are on display in the house, which dates to 1701.

Mohegan Indian Burial Ground (Norwich) This Native American resting place features a monument to Uncas, the noble Indian friend to Natty Bumppo in James Fenimore Cooper's famous novels of the early American frontier.

Mohegan Park and Memorial Rose Garden (Norwich) Fishing, swimming, walking the nature trails, and visiting the children's zoo are the most popular attractions in this nearly 380-acre park.

Mystic Marine Life Aquarium (Mystic) This aquarium is the state's largest, with 50 exhibits showing 6,000 living sea creatures, including seals, sea lions, and African black-footed penguins. Dolphin and whale demonstrations are presented daily at a marine theater that seats 1,400 people.

Mystic Seaport Museum (Mystic) This historical re-creation presents a glimpse of life in a nineteenth-century seaport. Its several exhibits, including period homes and shops, three ships, and a special Children's Museum, are spread over 17 acres.

Fort Griswold State Park (Groton) The park is on the site of the fortress captured by the traitor Benedict Arnold and the British during the Revolutionary War.

Submarine Force Library and Museum (Groton) Exhibits demonstrate how submarines developed and feature a model of Captain Nemo's *Nautilus* from Jules Verne's science-fiction novel, *Twenty Thousand Leagues Under the Sea*.

Connecticut River Museum (Essex) At this museum you will find exhibits of steamboats, shipbuilding, and regional archaeology. A popular exhibit highlights the *Turtle*, which was built in 1775 and is said to be the first submarine.

Beardsley Zoo (Bridgeport) Visitors can take a peek at 120 species of animals in outdoor habitats, visit an indoor rain forest exhibit, or pet the animals in the New England farm setting of the Children's Zoo.

Discovery Museum (Bridgeport) Interactive art and science exhibits, including the *Challenger* Learning Center and a planetarium, encourage visitors to explore their environment.

Monte Cristo Cottage (New London) The boyhood home of Eugene O'Neill was the setting for his famous play *Long Day's Journey into Night*.

Peabody Museum of Natural History (New Haven) Fossils of dinosaurs and prehistoric mammals are the attractions at this museum.

Eli Whitney Museum (Hamden) The numerous hands-on exhibits here include a water learning lab where visitors can operate valves and levers. A working model of the cotton gin is also on display, and a covered bridge and a waterfall beautify the grounds.

New Canaan Nature Center (New Canaan) Forty acres of plants and animals in their natural habitats, as well as a solar greenhouse, await visitors to the center.

Mattatuck Museum (Waterbury) Charles Goodyear's rubber desk is one of the highlights of this museum, devoted to the industrial history of the area.

The Institute for American Indian Studies (Washington) Indian artifacts chronicle 12,000 years of Native American life in this area. A replica of an Indian village, a nature trail, and an archaeological site offer further glimpses into Native American life.

New England Air Museum (Windsor Locks) Vintage and modern aircraft, as well as many different exhibits, will thrill aviation buffs of all ages.

Connecticut Fire Museum (East Windsor) offers a collection of antique fire equipment, including a fire sleigh, fire trucks, and memorabilia.

Connecticut Trolley Museum (East Windsor) Visitors can actually ride 3.75 miles on an antique trolley, as well as view all manner of trolleys and railroad cars dating from 1894 to 1947.

Lutz Children's Museum (Manchester) Hands-on exhibits about art, history, science, and nature make this museum unique. The 53-acre nature center features a variety of wildlife habitats, where visitors can see small native, domestic, and exotic animals.

Dinosaur State Park (Rocky Hill) More than 500 dinosaur footprints are on view at this geodome exhibit center, where visitors can make their own cast of an actual dinosaur footprint.

Harriet Beecher Stowe House (Hartford) The actual home of the famous abolitionist and author of *Uncle Tom's Cabin* offers a unique perspective on American history.

Mark Twain House (Hartford) Mark Twain made this Victorian Gothic mansion his home for 17 years. It was here that he wrote *Huckleberry Finn* and *Connecticut Yankee in King Arthur's Court*.

FIND OUT MORE

If you would like to find out more about Connecticut, look in your school library, local public library, bookstore, or video store for the following titles:

GENERAL STATE BOOKS

Bell, Michael. *The Face of Connecticut: People, Geology, and the Land.* Hartford: State Geological and Natural History Survey, 1985.

Boyle, Doe. *Connecticut Family Adventure Guide.* Old Saybrook, Conn.: The Globe Pequot Press, 1995.

Carpenter, Allan. *The New Enchantment of Connecticut.* Chicago: Childrens Press, 1979.

Gelman, Amy. *Connecticut.* Minneapolis: Lerner Publications, 1991.

Halliburton, Warren. *The People of Connecticut.* Norwalk, Conn.: Connecticut Yankee, 1984.

Hoyt, Joseph B. *The Connecticut Story.* New Haven: Readers Press, 1961.

Kent, Deborah. *America the Beautiful: Connecticut.* Chicago: Childrens Press, 1990.

BOOKS ABOUT CONNECTICUT PEOPLE, PLACES, OR HISTORY

Ash, Maureen. *The Story of Harriet Beecher Stowe.* Chicago: Childrens Press, 1990.

Barrett, Tracy. *Growing Up in Colonial America.* Brookfield, Conn.: Millbrook Press, 1995.

Cosner, Shaaron. *The Underground Railroad.* New York: Franklin Watts, 1991.

Faude, Wilson, and Joan W. Friedland. *Connecticut Firsts.* Old Saybrook, Conn.: Peregrine Press, 1985.

Fradin, Dennis Brindell. *The Connecticut Colony.* Chicago: Childrens Press, 1990.

Scott, John A. *John Brown of Harpers Ferry.* New York: Facts on File, 1988.

Soderlind, Arthur E. *Colonial Histories: Connecticut.* New York: Thomas Nelson, 1976.

WEBPAGE

On the Internet, you can find the State of Connecticut Home Page, which will have pictures, facts, and suggestions for further research about the state. Go to www.state.ct.us on the World Wide Web.

INDEX

Page numbers for illustrations are in boldface.